T0353698

THE
BEGINNER'S
GUIDE TO
METAPHYSICS

KIMBERLY A. JAMES

BALBOA.PRESS
A DIVISION OF HAY HOUSE

Balboa Press books may be ordered through booksellers or by contacting:

Balboa Press
A Division of Hay House
1663 Liberty Drive
Bloomington, IN 47403
www.balboapress.com
844-682-1282

Because of the dynamic nature of the Internet, any web addresses or links contained in this book may have changed since publication and may no longer be valid. The views expressed in this work are solely those of the author and do not necessarily reflect the views of the publisher, and the publisher hereby disclaims any responsibility for them.

The author of this book does not dispense medical advice or prescribe the use of any technique as a form of treatment for physical, emotional, or medical problems without the advice of a physician, either directly or indirectly. The intent of the author is only to offer information of a general nature to help you in your quest for emotional and spiritual well-being. In the event you use any of the information in this book for yourself, which is your constitutional right, the author and the publisher assume no responsibility for your actions.

Any people depicted in stock imagery provided by Getty Images are models, and such images are being used for illustrative purposes only. Certain stock imagery © Getty Images.

Print information available on the last page.

ISBN: 979-8-7652-5990-0 (sc)
ISBN: 979-8-7652-5989-4 (e)

Balboa Press rev. date: 03/27/2025

"An eye-opening, mystical and transcendental experience, which explores a deeper understanding of human existence through thought-provoking philosophical interpretations to elevate the awakening of one's consciousness."

CONTENTS

PREFACE

Although this may not be necessary for most, there is always the inevitable skeptic that will attempt to refute or diffuse the information contained herein. While any type of objective view is welcomed, the foregoing information is based upon over fifty years of research that began in early childhood. It is the hope of this author to provide some basic insight into our Earthly perspective of the Universe. As stated during every episode of *X-Files*, "The Truth Is Out There!"

On a secondary note, it is incredibly unfortunate that our society has, for centuries, thwarted not only the ability to gain discernment on planet Earth, but also the Universe in which we live. Children marvel at their existence on Earth and without question or doubt. It is only the conditioning of those in "power"[1] that inhibits our natural openness. We all hail from one Source. As we begin our journey from the Third Dimensional realm of existence and ascend to a higher level of consciousness, the Fifth Dimension, those in "power" will no longer be able to hinder our perception of "reality."

Ascension is not an easy task during what appears to be the dire straits of human existence – the times in which we currently live. To the advanced soul, transmutation is only "understood" because it is recognized early in life. "When a soul not in teaching encounters the true personality in essence for the first time, it is, of course, a devastating experience", which is usually the result of "...extreme stress grief, or

---

[1] The word power is in quotations for a specific reason. No one person can control another unless *permitted*. Living in fear is a great form of control. Be mindful of this every single day.

sometimes even trauma" (Yarboro, p. 65). Transitioning from the Third Dimension to the Fifth will take effort. Many may find themselves disheartened. At present, transitioning is mandatory in order for humans to evolve. Enjoy the journey, the destination will be well worth every attempt, big or small.

INTRODUCTION

It should be noted that the ultimate goal of this project - *The Beginner's Guide to Metaphysics* - is to broaden one's perspective and provide opportunities to expand one's consciousness, and not just individually, or even globally, but on a galactic level. While one's journey may differ in outlook and approach via their specific set of social mores and ethnicity, the human race is *one* and the *same*. There is no room for "racial" or gender discrimination, only unity. The society in which we live (referring to the United States of America) has thwarted our ability to look beyond daily life by creating an atmosphere of competition that creates discord. Innovation comes from imagination, which can only be incorporated into consciousness when we collaborate. Metaphysics opens one's consciousness through the ability to see the complexity of human nature. Understanding and welcoming the diversity on Earth adds to the beauty of human existence.

The world in which we live is based upon metaphysics. The Greeks considered metaphysics to be one of the branches of philosophy. Merriam-Webster defines metaphysics as "a division of philosophy that is concerned with the *fundamental nature of reality and being...*" [emphasis added], which also includes the study of ontology, cosmology and epistemology. While *physics* is based upon our three dimensional existence and concerns the nature of matter and energy, the prefix *meta* refers to going beyond nature and the origin of reality itself.

To better understand the metaphysical realm, it is best to briefly describe the three other philosophical branches; ontology, cosmology and epistemology, as defined by the Merriam-Webster dictionary. Ontology is "...an abstract philosophical study of what is outside objective experience."

Cosmology is "...a branch of astronomy that deals with the origin, structure, and space-time relationships of the universe." Lastly, epistemology is "...the study or a theory of the nature and grounds of knowledge especially with reference to its limits and validity." In essence, all metaphysical components are intertwined and create a cohesive whole. (See Merriam-Webster.)

Metaphysics has a very wide base. This *Beginner's Guide* will focus on several metaphysical topics, or themes of existence, but is by no means all encompassing. The pages to come will provide a basic and foundational understanding of all the subject matter included. By having basic knowledge of each, the opportunity to hone in on a specific subject that resonates with one's understanding of the universe will become clear. In order to assist with the journey, a list of potential books, videos and websites will be provided at the end of the book under "References & Additional Sources." These reference points are a jump start toward personal topic(s) of interest. Hopefully, each topic will assist with one's personal journey, along with a deeper understanding of human nature, as well as the many mysteries of the universe.

It should also be noted that the world is moving towards a deeper level of consciousness. While living in this Third Dimensional reality those born after October 1971 through present day have a different approach to life, which began when Pluto presented itself in the sign of Libra. The ultimate goal of the 21st Century is to raise our awareness to a Fifth Dimensional reality. "When we develop ourselves along this line, this world will be much better place to live..." (Ward, p. 70). According to Margarete Ward, well-renowned writer of the fortune telling game of "Gong Hee Fot Choy," this process is an opening of our sixth sense, also referred to as the communication through mental telepathy. This is also reflective of our innate psychic abilities, for which every human has bestowed at the moment of their birth. Ward imparts this information in her original publication, which occurred in 1948. Ward's first awakening was nearly 75 years ago, making our Ascension as a species long overdue. Ward adds that once we open our hearts and minds to this awareness, "...we will be able to commune with...loved ones that are taking a spiritual rest" (p. 70). Notably, those with whom have passed away and exist in alternate dimensions. Through meditation and relaxation, one will no longer need an intermediary.

Lastly, the information contained herein has been a collaborative effort. The many experts listed and quoted have been utilized to emphasize this author's content. Much of the information has been channeled through past life recall, accessing of the Akashic Records and willing cosmic participants.

Let your journey begin!

CHAPTER 1

CHAKRAS

This chapter is dedicated to the concept of "Chakras," which is pronounced "shaa · kruhz." It is difficult to ascertain the exact time that the development of this ancient, complex, energetic and spiritual system began. The word *chakra* is derived from the Sanskrit word *wheel* and relates to the energy fields of the body. Buddhism is noted to have a five wheel system, while Hinduism has seven, both of which are intertwined with one's aura. The *"aura"* is the energetic, electromagnetic field found in every living thing on Earth, which surrounds the body via a spectrum of color, known to radiate about three to five feet from the body. The auric field, and the amount of feet that surrounds the body, is dependent upon one's soul evolution. The more one transmutes, the larger their auric field. According to expert Cyndi Dale, chakras are the "vehicles of consciousness" that represent light, color and frequency.[2] Modern day philosopher and spiritual guide, Matias de Stephano, in his lecture series "Initiation" on Gaia television, takes this one step further by introducing nine energetic fields. Many experts discuss the seven energetic fields that run along the human spine. De Stephano includes both the feet and the knees, which relate to the extremities of the human body.

As we are all energetic beings, plants and animals included, metaphysics can not be properly understood without a basic knowledge of "energy." Obviously, this is a subject matter that is incredibly vast. The study of energy, or *"energeia,"* was initially understood by the Greeks in the 4th

---

[2] "Chakras: Beyond the Basics with Cyndi Dale" (2017) on *Open Minds* with Regina Meredith: Season 10, Episode 7.

Century BCE[3] by Aristotle, then officially coined by Thomas Young in 1802 at a lecture held by the Royal Society (Wikipedia. "History of Energy"). Since that time frame, a multitude of experiments have been conducted with comprehensive data obtained and analyzed by both physicists and quantum physicists. Energy is the ability to do work and, according to Einstein, is interchangeable with matter; "they are different forms of the same thing."[4] The result – "[m]atter is the material substance that constitutes the observable universe and, together with energy, forms the basis of all objective phenomena" (Britannica.com). Author of "The Prism of Lyra," Lyssa Royal-Holt, defines matter as "...densified energy vibrating at a specific rate," and states that "[e]very aspect of the universe is made up of energy" (p. 3).

The latest quantum understanding is very different than what was initially thought to be true. It was believed that matter was made up of particles or waves. Quantum physicists, through a variety of evidence-based studies, now believe "...matter is more fundamentally made up of energy fragments..." that come in the form [of] solids, liquids or gaseous materials (Silverberg, L. M. & Eischen, J. 2020). At their base, solids, liquids and gases are made of tiny particles called atoms and molecules. At its basic core, energy is a property of matter and manifests in many forms. According According to the article *"Earth and Matter: Flows, Cycles and Conversations"* found on Exploring Our Fluid Earth website, "...both energy and matter are conserved within a system. This means that energy and matter can change forms but cannot be created or destroyed. Energy and matter are often cycled within a system, and different forms of matter and energy are able to interact." This definition implies that energy mutates or morphs into another form. Furthermore, energy is dynamic, not static. Humans are comprised of energy, atoms that form molecules, but also have consciousness, which is the *awareness* of being "human" (a/k/a, the soul!), while matter portrays the physical body. Additionally, energy can neither be created nor destroyed, it simply *IS*; therefore, *we* as humans–conscious energy–can only change form, making "death" *only* a three dimensional reality.

Aside from the subject of energy, a short note on meditation is also

[3] BCE: Before Common Era.
[4] Quote from "Einstein's Big Idea" as seen on Nova via PBS.

warranted. Meditation refers to an active practice of contemplation or a quieting of the mind, and works in tandem with chakra healing. There are a myriad of books and videos that take one through healing in relation to chakras, as well as other areas of personal interest. All spiritual teachers agree that daily meditation is a standard practice for one's well being. Conventional meditation may be difficult for some individuals. The ultimate purpose is to reach theta brain-wave frequencies, which in turn cause one's attentions to the outer world and all other distractions to dissipate. According to Dr. Joe Dispenza in his book "Becoming Supernatural; How Uncommon People Are Doing the Uncommon," the real point is "...to disconnect your association to all the elements in your outer environment..." and go beyond the body, fears, and responsibilities of day-to-day life (p. 54). The reward is the ability to call energy back and recenter oneself. Don't give up. Look at alternative methods for quieting the mind, such as simple deep breathing exercise. Speaking from experience, this singular technique helps with the daily stressors of life. A new technique for parenting also includes a similar concept: When experiencing discord with a child, count to ten before taking action. Slowing down a reaction allows for a clearer view and mindset. This, in turn, presents a more positive disciplinary outcome. Actually, this is a good practice for all age groups. It helps to let go of the ego reaction.

New York Times best-selling author Dr. Joe Dispenza walks through chakra energy, how such energies work within the brain and are all interconnected with our emotional well-being. Throughout the book, and specifically on page 101 under *Figure 4.4B*, he explains that "[w]hen energy becomes stuck in our body, it cannot flow to the higher centers. Since emotions are energy, these emotions get stuck in different centers...", stopping the evolutionary process. This information alone indicates the importance of becoming aware of one's energetic field. There are a myriad of meditation books and practices targeting the specific areas of the body to promote clarity, increased emotional understanding and healing.

According to Hinduism, the seven energetic fields run along the human spine, connecting with specific organs and glands that pertain to various fields of energy, as well as one's emotional make-up. De Stephano[5] includes both the feet and the knees, which appear to relate to flexibility and movement (muscle-skeletal systems) within the human body. Each of these nine main chakras has a corresponding name, color identifier, specific location and meaning. The "+" and "–" aspects of the chart represent what occurs when a specific Chakra is either "open" (+) or "closed" (–).

Chart No. 1.1

CHAKRAS

NAME	LOCATION	COLOR	MEANING	
Crown	Above Head	Violet	**Key Word is *Mentalism*.** Controls both the brain, nervous system and connects all Chakra systems into a cohesive whole.	
			+	Higher capacity for Spirituality and Enlightenment.
			–	Exhibit narrow-mindedness, skepticism or stubbornness.
Third Eye	Center of Forehead	Indigo	**Key Word is *Correspondence*.** An Ability to Connect.	
			+	Intuition and Imagination.
			–	Issues with Sight, Concentration and Hearing.
Throat	Throat	Blue	**Key word is *Vibration*.**	
			+	Excellent Communication Skills with Ability to Express Self Clearly.
			–	Issues around Dominating Conversations, Gossip, Speaking without Thinking and Difficulty Speaking One's Mind.

[5] "Key Words" (Chakra Nos. 1-7) relate to those expressed by Matias de Stephano in his lecture series "Initiation" (2019); Season 1, Episode 7; Numbers 8-9 represent authors take.

Chart No. 1.1

CHAKRAS

Heart	Center of Chest	Green		**Key Word is *Rhythm*.** Rhythm is connected to time.
			+	Loving, Compassionate and Empathetic to Everything and Everyone.
			−	A Closed Heart Doesn't Allow Self-Love. Health Issues Manifest as Heart Problems, Asthma and Weight Gain.
Solar Plexis	Upper Abdomen	Yellow		**Key Words are *Cause & Effect*.**
			+	Self Confidence, Self-Esteem and Stability w/out Ego. Someone Who Holds Everything Together
			−	Relates to Digestive Problems – Heartburn, Eating Disorders, Indigestion.
Sacral	Below Belly Button	Orange		**Key Word is *Polarity*.**
			+	Connected to Feelings of Self-Worth Around One's Sexuality and Creativity.
			−	Blockages Manifest as Urinary Tract Infections, Impotency and Lower Back Pain.
Root	Base of Spine	Red		**Key Word is *Generation*.**
			+	Safety, Security and Grounding. Sexual Center.
			−	Initial fight or flight response is a necessity; however, it can be taken to an extreme, causing physical and emotional paralysis. Arthritis, constipation and sexual anxiety, confusion, depravity and addiction are indicative of blockage.

Chart No. 1.1

CHAKRAS

Flexion	Knees	Burgundy	**Key Word is *Flexibility*.** + Without the knee joints, the body would have no flexibility, making walking very awkward. − Knee issues can relate to an inflexibility somewhere within one's psyche. Although a physician will claim "old age," where no injury has occurred, it is really linked to an inflexibility in one's life. If lack of flexion is present, it would behoove one to determine exactly where in life lack of flexibility is present.
Base	Feet	Magenta	**Key Word is *Movement*.** + Without feet, the body would have little, if any, free movement, thus the "base." While the Root Chakra relates to stability, it is on an emotional level. − Where are you blocked with free movement?

Although extensive research did not present a nine Chakra system, it is logical. It is also this author's understanding that the Chakra system is really based around twelve tiers with the twelfth level considered Source energy. The arms and hands representing the tenth and eleventh with the twelfth sitting above the crown Chakra and encompassing all the eleven to bring one into their own spherical realm known as one's *essence*. Throughout life, it has always been a huge question mark: Why does the first chakra commence at the "root" or at the base of the spine and not at the base of the human? Additionally, many healers, including Shaman, Reiki practitioners and massage therapists, utilize their hands to radiate healing energy.

It should also be noted that color has a specific vibrational frequency. As such, the colors for which one is attracted can have calming and healing effects, even overwhelming feelings of love and compassion. Those involved in the healing arts, including sound bath practitioners, massage therapists,

Reiki healers, Rolfing practitioners, Shiatsu and Swedish massage practitioners, and the like, also work with energy. Specific techniques utilized by each type of practitioner differ. Not every practitioner's approach will suit every individual. Like meditation, therapy of any kind is very personal; however, all have the same intention: Bringing one back to their center.

CHAPTER 2

PALMISTRY

Reading a hand is like reading a book – The Book of You! Like many practices, reading one's palm has no set date upon which its beginnings can be traced. It may also be considered a type of "divination;" however, it is truly a singular, very *personal* reading, unlike others that will be explored later. After all, there is only one hand in the whole world like yours. It contains specific information about your strengths, talents, personality traits, health and even how you feel about yourself. It also speaks about weaknesses and the characteristics needed to be developed to become a well-rounded person. It shows the work and life-style choices that are likely to bring the most fulfillment, and reveals periods of ease or challenges over the course of one's life. The most interesting facet is that only one hand changes, the dominant or active one. The recessive hand does not change; it shows the pattern given at birth, the gifts and challenges of the soul's journey. The dominant hand represents the present and the future but never one's fate. You are the co-creator of your life with the *free will* to alter your circumstances.

Reading palms can be extensive. Every part of the hand has a corresponding meaning, which even includes the shapes of one's fingers and size and shape of one's hand. There are specific sections on all the fingers and the palm that relate to the planets within our solar system. The Mount of Venus, situated at the soft tissue area near the thumb in an oval shape and ending at the boundary of the Life Line, is the most prominent mount, and when certain symbols or designs are present, it signifies psychic or intuitive gifts.

In simpler form, the palm is broken down into specific lines that relate to life categories. Diagram No. 2.1 (below) shows the true intricacies of Palmistry.

Diagram No. 2.1

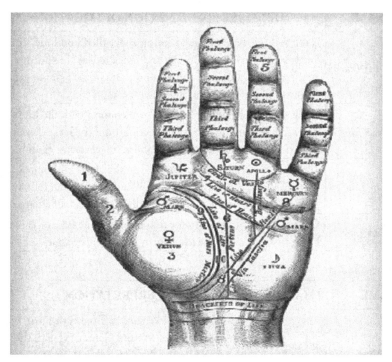

Palmistry "Palm" depicting all lines and facets of hand.

Chart No. 2.1 introduces the name and location of the pronounced lines with a detailed description. *Chart Nos. 2.2 – 2.4* will provide the variety of actual meanings. Every hand is different; therefore, the lines may be shorter or longer, deeper or faint. According to Cassandra Eason's book, "A Little Bit of Palmistry: An Introduction to Palm Reading," it is also possible to gauge timing of life events. Page 12 of Eason's book notes that in the simplest form, by age 35, the Fate Line reaches the Head line, by age 49, the Fate Line reaches the Heart Line and the remainder of the palm signifies the period towards the end of one's life (Eason, 2018).

Chart No. 2.1

NAME	DETAILED EXPLANATION OF LOCATION
Heart Line	Is the first line below fingers, falling above the Head Line. This line begins between the middle and index fingers, often times curving downward and running to the end of the palm towards the small finger. The opposite of the Head Line.
Head Line	Is the second (or middle) line, and can connect with the Life Line. It is read in the opposite direction from the Heart line, from the small finger towards the index finger and/or thumb.
Life Line	The Life Line is generally connected to the Head Line but can also fall above. Reading begins below index finger and follows downwards toward the wrist, generally creating a half circular.
Fate Line	Generally Runs from index or ring fingers to the Base of Palm. Not every person will have a Fate or multiple Fate Lines.

Chart No. 2.2

NAME	FORMATION	INTERPRETATION
Heart Line	Clear, Deep & Long	Deep Emotional Person, In Tune with Own Emotional Awareness and Concerned with the Needs of Others. Problem Solver.
	Faint	Low Energy Field, Sensitive and Prone to Being Bullied.
	Pale, Flat & Broad	Sentimental but Expresses a Peaceful Emotional Nature.
	Long, Curved Line	Follows Desires & Passions. Can Be Romantically Impulsive.
	Short & Straight	Demonstrates Love Through Action, Non-Demonstrative, Practical; therefore, Non-Romantic.
	Curved @ End	Ability to Express Both Inner Feelings and Needs.
	Without Curve	Tendency to be Sensitive & Easily Hurt; Requires Affection.
	Beginning at or Slightly Left of Middle Finger	Indicates Balance in Relationships.
	Merges with Head Line	Love Relationship and Business Relationship would be a Successful Combination.

	Close to Base of Fingers with Wide Space	A Person Who is Non-Responsive with Cold Interactions.
	Consistently Broken, Several Branches	Initially Exhibit Intense Feelings for People; Very Idealistic.

It should also be noted that the Heart Line has several additional meanings not initially mentioned on page 10. For instance, if two people's hands are similar, especially those of partners, then strong compatibility is indicated. It is also a nearly infallible marker that they share many previous incarnations together. A line that splits in two reveals a person who puts the needs of others first, while splitting into a trident (3 lines) demonstrates luck in both love and life. Lastly, a consistently chained (∞∞) line infers more than one love relationship occurring simultaneously, potentially conflicting emotions or past life/unfinished karmic business. Remember, one's hand can and does alter, more frequently for some than others. While a chain may appear at one point in one's lifetime, it can, and often does, disappear.

According to Eason, the Head Line is an expression of "...how our thoughts and intellect are manifest in our lives; our logic and rational dealings with the world and those around us..." (p. 9).

Chart No. 2.3

NAME	FORMATION	INTERPRETATION
Head Line	Long, Well-Formed	A Person Who Believes in Justice and Idealism.
	Deep	Concentration and Memorization Come Easy.
	Faint	Not Utilizing Intellectual and Reasoning Capabilities.
	Short	Fast Thinker, Unlimited Capacity for Non-Traditional Learning.
	Pale & Short	Timid Personality, Difficulty with Decision Making.
	Straight Line	Practical Approach to Life; If Extends to Little Finger, Overly Analytical.
	Continual Straight Line Across Palm	Pragmatic, Good Business Sense and Persistent.
	Split Line	Ability to See Both Sides or a Person Who Sits on the Fence.

Touches Life Line at Start	A Person Who Thinks Before s/he Acts.
Begins @ Mount of Jupiter[6]	Great Teacher or Instructor. Possibly Influenced by Ambitions.
Curves Toward Wrist	Creative an Imaginative Approach. Able to Find Alternative Solutions to Difficult or Perplexing Problems.
Below Life Line	Shy Personality, Possible Grew-Up with Absent Parent, Hidden Insecurities.
Upward Branches	Skilled Money Making Abilities.
Forks @ End	Excellent Written and/or Skilled at Communicating.
Double Head Line	Person is a Genius, Double-Dealer or both.

Before continuing on to the next section, the length of any one line, including the Life Line, does not represent "measurement." As expressed previously, psychics and/or mediums are not privy to any one persons date of death. Eason suggests that while attempting to predict the future, "...the most useful function of palmistry..." should be based upon "...new lines either of independence or [of] new love [that] become smooth and deep..." (page 13). These new, yet subtle, changes are strong illustration of the potential of future events, which should also be analyzed against the non-dominant hand.

The Life Line is not indicative of whether or not one has control over their own destiny. It is evidence of how to better understand one's own life purpose. The actual amount that the Life Line encircles on the palm also has great significance.

Chart No. 2.4

NAME	FORMATION	INTERPRETATION
	Encircles Wide Base	Great Stamina and Energy. An Adventurous Person who is Willing to Seize the Day.
	Hugs Thumb	Demonstrates a Person Who Exhibits Listlessness.
	Starts Closer to Thumb	Laid Back and Carefree Approach.

---

[6] See Diagram 2.1, Page 1.

Life Line	Straight	Cautious and Reserved in Relationships and Life's Challenges.
	Long, Well-Defined	High Achiever but Compassionate in Nature.
	Unbroken & Smooth	Relatively Smooth Sailing Throughout Life.
	Dips or Curves Sharply @ Base of Palm	Many Opportunities Presented Throughout Life to Take New Paths that Prove Worthwhile.
	Short	Easily Manipulated.
	Very Short	"Momentous changes caused by external events." (Eason, p. 21)
	Deep	Exhibit Strong Feelings and Embrace Life Experiences.
	Forks	Scattered and Wasted Energy. Need for Balance.
	Chains Throughout	Many Options and Choices Presented Throughout Life.

Fate or Destiny Lines are generally light or faint and present vertically, midway between the mount of the Moon and Mount of Venus toward the Line of Saturn (See Diagram 2.1); however, not every person will have them. They can run through all of the major lines (Head, Heart, Life), from the top of middle finger to the bottom near the wrist, and appear to be more prone toward explaining life's unexpected challenges rather than actual luck. Straight Fate Lines are noted to show one's focus in relation to life plans, "...whereas a wavering Fate line could suggest the path of someone who spends time exploring or searching for the best-fitting life purpose to undertake..." (Eason, p. 22). They can appear later in life, in one's twenties or thirties. As one's purpose becomes more solid, the waves will become straighter, making one's life path more clear and developed. If a Faint Line is noted in childhood, it usually implies that the child will follow in the footsteps of a family member (e.g., military career, teacher, doctor, etc.). This particular occurrence would make for fabulous research over a long period of time.

Chart No. 2.5

NAME	FORMATION	INTERPRETATION
Fate / Destiny Line	Absent	Very Strong Past Life & Karmic Influences. Notification to Stop Repeating Old Patterns.
	Joined to Life Line	Captain of Your Own Ship.
	Long Link w/ Life Line	Close to Family; however, May Feel Undue Obligations or Guilt.
	Away From Life Line	Early Independence.
	Faint	Drifting Through Life with No Clear Path. "Feeling at the Mercy of Fate..." Rather than Having Opportunities or Choices (Eason, p. 24)
	Forked	Two Alternative Career Choices, which are Dependent upon Other Decisions Made, or Not, During Life.
	Ends on Heart Line	May Give up Career for Love or Searching for Other Life Fulfillment(s).
	Ends on Head Line	Set in Career and Lifestyle by Middle Age. Faint Line Indicates Potential Career Burnout.
	Deep	Controlled by Destiny.[7]
	Clear, Deep, Unwavering	Competitive Nature (Career & Sports). Strives to Achieve the Best. Prone to do Whatever it Takes to Succeed.
	Very Pale & Wavy *or* Disappearing Sections	Influenced by Others, Causing Discouragement and Belief in Oneself.
	Broken	Career Disruptions, unless Continues in Different Locale, New Career Path.
	Ends @ Jupiter	"Gifted in Politics, Religion, Law, Teaching..." (Eason, p. 25).
	Ends @ Saturn	"Exceptional destiny...", Adept Psychic and/or Material Success. (Eason, p. 25).
	Ends @ Apollo	Creative, Artistic and/or Writing Abilities.

---

[7] "Destiny" is really one's own agreement(s) made prior to each incarnation. See "Michael" and "Reincarnation" sections.

Other areas of interest in Palmistry include the Fortune Line, the Health Line, the Intuition Line, the Line of Mars, the Line of Money, Travel Lines, Marriage Lines and Children Lines. As the "Marriage Lines" and "Children Lines" are of great importance to most humans, it behooves inclusion within this *Beginner's Guide*. The Marriage Line(s) fall between the Heart Line and the Mercury (pinky) finger. Traditionally, the right hand relates to women (Divine Feminine), the left hand is read for men (Divine Masculine), and the number of marriages; however, if the person for whom the reading is being conducted is in a long-term, heart centered marriage (or commitment), any other lines present can relate to a very close, lifelong friendship(s) or deep connectedness to a family member. Lines reflecting the number of children correspond to the vertical lines within the same area and may cross the marriage line. According to Eason, "[f]or a man, children lines [indicate] that a man will be a good father, have good relations professionally or with stepchildren" (p. 41). Lastly, one must not forget that not all "children" come from the actual woman whose hand is being read, but can relate to surrogacy, adoption and foster care.

The last part of this chapter includes other types of markings on the palms and information that has been handed down to the author via family members and mentors. *Chart No. 2.5* illustrates the specific "Markings" found on the hand, while *Chart No. 2.6* represents markings by way of lines rather than shapes. With regard to the knowledge passed down, the first and most interesting detail concerns human stubbornness. To test this with friends and family, hold the palm outward and push the thumb downward. One thumb should suffice but checking both will truly exhibit the degree of stubbornness presented within the individual. If the thumb bounces back, stubbornness is not an issue; however, if the thumb doesn't bounce and is fairly immobile, the person for whom the reading is being done has stubborn tendencies. With regard to fingers, any one or more finger that shows an inclination toward being bent or curved at the tip is an implication that this person is either not truthful, has been very dishonest in past lives or both. Oddly, stress levels can be measured by putting the two palms, pinky side together, and lining them up at the bottom line of the fingers. If the fingers do not match at the top, it is a sign that this person is experiencing stress and a course correction via meditation or other means is warranted.

Chart No. 2.6

NAME	FORMATION		INTERPRETATION
Markings	Chains	∞∞	Obstacles. If Shown on Non-Dominant Hand = Past-Life Conflicts.
		♥ Line	Earlier Setbacks in Regard to Love Interests. Can also be Indicative of an Overly Emotional and Possessive Personality or a Tendancy Toward Co-Dependency in Relationships.
		♣ Line	Distractions. Too Many Irons in the Fire, Leading to Inability to Complete Necessary Projects, even Daily Tasks.
	Islands	●	Unfavorable Interruptions (Eason, p. 84).
		♥ Line	"Unresolved Emotional Issues" from Childhood, Resulting in Trust Issues (Eason, p. 84).
		Life Line	Indication of Depression, Most Likely Related to Daily Stressors.
		Fate Line	Financial Stress.
	Squares	■	Indicates Luck, "...[e]specially...after a triangle...", which Enhances Strength and Good Fortune (Eason, p. 84).

Chart No. 2.7

NAME	FORMATION		INTERPRETATION
Markings by Way of Lines	Worry Lines		These Manifest by Fine Horizontal Lines, Generally Found on the Mount of Venus between the Thumb and Life Line. The More Lines Present, the Greater the "Worry-Wart!" Meditation, Sound Baths, Nature Walks and Counseling are Extremely Beneficial to the alleviation of stress.
	Crosses	✝, X	Contrary to What these Symbols Represent to Some, on the Palm, Crosses Signify Major Changes that are Positive in Nature. It's Like Solar and/or Lunar Eclipses. For Those Who Stay Stagnant, not Living up to Their Potential, these Will Manifest as an Opportunity to Reverse Current Actions.
	Grills	## ##	More Typically Found on "Mounts," Grills Represent the Need for Freedom. The Location is Indicative of Where One is Being Stifled. By Properly Identifying the Source or Cause of Such Discomfort, One Can Release the Negative or Crippling Patterns of Behavior to Find that Much Needed Liberation. According to Eason, "Grills are very responsive to pendulum healing (p. 86).
	Dots or Spots	□	Dots or Spots are Filled-in and Located Anywhere. If Found on Worry Lines, Concerns Around Health, Job Loss or Failed Relationships Could Be Possible. Resolve Comes Through Different Means. If Ignoring Health Problems, Seek Advice from a Health Care Professional. If Relationship Trouble is Present, Perhaps Taking a Deep Dive into a Heart Felt Conversation on with One's Partner, Personal Therapy or Couples Counseling Should Be Considered.
	Stars	*	Ending at a Specific Line Implies Total Success in Relation to the Line. Celebrity or Media Success are Alluded to When a Star is Situated on Mount of the Moon, while a Star on the Mount of Jupiter (Below Index Finger) or Saturn (Below Middle Finger) Suggest Public Office.

Tassels		According to Eason, Tassels or Frayed Lines Infer "[t]emporary confusion, or an impasse linked to the relevant line or mount..." but tend to "...disappear rapidly once the confusion is cleared..." (p.88). Eason Advises that One Should Evaluate the Locale and Situation and take a "...step back if chaos is coming from someone else"(Eason, p. 88).
Triangles		Considerable Luck and Success at Area Where Positioned. When Situated on the Mount of Saturn or the Moon, One is both a Psychic and a Healer with Potential Career Opportunities in Media. The Mount of Mercury or Apollo Indicates a "...razor-sharp mind, promising financial, scientific or business success and recognition...," which can even be on an international level (Eason, p. 88). Lastly, a Small Triangle within the Center of the Palm indicates Money is Earned via One's Abilities.
Great Triangles		"A more permanent marking created by the conjunction of the Life, Head and Fate or Health lines, a sign of lifetime success" (Eason, p. 89).
Tridents		Brings Life of Luck and Happiness in Health and Financially. When Pointed Downward, Be Careful NOT to Take Life or Good Fortune/Luck for Granted.

CHAPTER 3

NUMEROLOGY

Numbers are the true language of the universe. Some say, the universal language of Source. ALL civilizations understand the language of numbers. One is always "1," two is always "2," and so on. That is why mathematicians can communicate amongst themselves without the necessity of speaking the same written language. At birth, the numbers system is set in motion. Your birth month, day and year have a frequency that corresponds with your "angelic" number, setting forth the tone of your current life's vibrational frequency. The specific "day" of your birth holds the most substantial frequency and sets-forth your archetype (or archetypes) that will present throughout your current incarnation. The name is also very important as it has a unique, personal vibration. Every written language has a specific base number assigned to each letter. The actual number is designated at birth and calculated via the use of your full legal name given by your parent(s). If a choice is made to change your legal name due to marriage, or perhaps just a personal choice, that will change your vibrational frequency.

Many people literally see numbers in every part of matter. Could this be a more direct form of communicating with Source and, in succession, also the Earth? Number sequences also have a particular resonance with certain people. When a combination of numbers presents itself, it can be an indication of communication from Spirits outside 3D existence. For instance, the sequential numbers "444" and "11:11" are universally known to represent communication from angels. Often during difficult times, the numbers "444" will present, either via a digital clock or through license plate numbers. This helps redirect energy toward the "greater good," and the understanding that Source is ever present. When one experiences number sequencing, especially repeating patterns in triplicate strewn over days, even weeks, pay attention. "Someone" is trying to communicate with you. Most likely your guardian angel.

As specified above, each number represents a specific vibrational frequency that also coincides with the archetype, or archetypes, you are attempting to master in your current incarnation. There are, however, a few schools that represent differences in thought. Some numerologists believe the specific number sequences of "11" and "22" have additional vibrational flare due to their double digitizing natures. A sort of exhaulted view. The Greeks believed those born specifically on the "11" or "22" day of the month were "masters;" those born with a higher level of awareness and, therefore, demonstrated a higher level of consciousness. Others believe, while an emphasis may be warranted, the base birthday numbers are still 2 (1+1) and 4 (2+2), respectively. As numbers, which coincide with patterned geometrical shapes, have been the mainstay of existence, the base number is what is considered the "standard." Additionally, numbers correspond with specific archetypes, *all* of which are represented in the Major Arcana of the Tarot deck, for which there are a total of "22," but represented as "0" through "21." If your birthday falls between a 1 and 9, your archetype will be rather straight forward. Birthdays ranging from 10 – 22 will utilize each single digit number represented by a Tarot archetype, as well as the combination of the whole. The *Major Arcana* will be covered more thoroughly under *Chapter 7*, and represents "The Tarot," wherein a more refined definition of each archetype will be provided.

The name given at birth is known to set the tone of one's lifetime. Mystical and metaphysical doctrines believe all words have resonance, creating vibrational power. "Through the Law of Correspondence, under the guidelines of The Seven Laws of the Universe, a name contains within it the power of choice" (Numerology.com). "[W]hen analyzed using arithmetic methods...," an understanding is created, assisting one with "... how to best empower...actions so that they result" in the desired effects (Numerology.com). This is when the number 11, 22 and 33 have their greatest influences, especially when it comes to one's middle name. Many numerologists believe the middle name has the most influence in one's life, primarily because it represents your inner expression or true essence.

A basic chart representing the numbers 1–9 is provided. If you were born between the tenth and thirty-first of a particular month break down your number into its primary form. If born on the eleventh or twenty-second, it is an indication that you have achieved "master" status. The "master" of exactly "what," is personal and, therefore, only you will know the correct answer to "what."

Ex.1: *Birthday*: September 24, 1963.
First number sequence is 9^8 + 2 + 4 + 1 + 9 + 6 + 3 = 34. 3 + 4 = **7.**
The actual day of birth is even more relevant: 2 + 4 = **6.**

Ex2: There was a video that presented itself recently during some YouTube visits concerning the frequency and vibration of Earth. According to "Stef," the creator and owner of "AstralHQ," the Earth vibrates at a specific level of 432 Mega-Hertz. In numerology, all numbers are reduced to their base number. For example, 432 breaks down to 4+3+2 = 9. We have a base "10" system that begins with "0." Although not a "Conspiracy Theorist" by nature, Stef discusses in his video that those in power have adjusted our frequency (via cell towers, cell phones, computers, etc.) as a form of mind control, setting the vibrational frequency to 440 Mega-Hertz, which effects the human body very negatively.

As we live in a system that is set-forth in polarity (positive and negative "energy"), each viewpoint has been provided. The goal is to always find that delicate balance between the two. The purpose of utilizing numerology in your life is to help better understand your character and that of others. It is "divination" at its core. Other personality traits, especially those contained within both Chinese and Western astrology, can help to dissipate negative aspects of your base numbers (full birth date, actual day and name). Human's, after all, are multidimensional beings.

---

[8] September being the ninth month of the year.

#		DESCRIPTION
1 *PIONEER*	+	Represents new beginnings or a new cycle, which makes those with this number ambitious pioneers. Always looking towards the "newest" innovation and/or technology, etc. They are natural born leaders, seeking to unify in all areas of life. They exude independence, confidence and self-determination, which affords great opportunities throughout life.
	−	While they exhibit an essence of very strong-will, the flip side means they can be stubborn and selfish. The extreme version, without self-control, causes obstinate behavior. Some may exhibit risky behaviors, the flip side being a "pioneer." An inability to see another persons point of view can also be a negative aspect.
2 *DUALITY*	+	Represents the concept of duality and femininity. Often times "2's" need partnerships, both personal and professional, in order to fully understand themselves. This number also represents grace, peace, harmony, balance and teamwork. Two individuals have a strong sense of intuition. According to "Numerology.com," [t]he 2 holds a tremendous amount of power over situations and relationships (love and otherwise) but handles it so carefully that its influence can go almost undetected. It's like it's working behind the scenes: no one sees it happening, but the results are undeniable. It does not have to push or use force with others because its incredible abilities of compassion and cooperation influence them to follow its guidance."
	−	The opposition of the number "2," in general, should be straight forward: A "2" may have difficulty being alone. Also, the ego can also pose an issue when credit is not always given where due, causing some internal conflict.
3 *TRINITY*	+	Represents the "trinity." Under specific religious viewpoints, which are primarily concerned with Catholics, Lutherans, Greek Orthodox, Russian Orthodox and Presbyterians, the trinity is symbolic for "the father, the son, the holy spirit." To the Greeks, the number 3 represented perfection and symbolized harmony, wisdom and understanding. In mathematics, it represents the geometric shape of a triangle. Triangles in ancient cultures symbolized the base of existence in the physical realm. Three is also associated with mysticism and there are many cultural observations found throughout all societies that intertwine: *a.* birth-life-death; *b.* "good things come in 3's; *c.* mind-body-soul, etc. This number 3 person is highly original and creative, communicative, loyal, optimistic, sincere and trustworthy. They have a zest for life and are considered upbeat and charming.
	−	A few of the negative aspects may present as disorganization and/or difficulty committing to one hobby or career path. The 3 person can also be naive, unfocused and a bit shallow. After all, having fun is their first priority.

#	DESCRIPTION
4 *ELEMENTS* *of NATURE*	+ Initially, the number 4 is representative of the elements: Earth, Water, Fire ad Air. Also the Earth's seasons and the cardinal directions; north, south, east and west. Four lines create a square, which then geometrically morphs into a cube. There are 13 annual lunar cycles. The number 4 person is concerned with family and home life. They seek balance, harmony and wholeness within their home life. The 4 person is a supportive force that provides stability. They are also commitment oriented. In essence, each side of the square connects to the physical, mental, emotional and spiritual aspects of life. – As the four person loves their home, they have a tendency to be "homebodies," which can translate into lacking an adventurous spirit. Achieving "balance," is often times easier said than done. There is a delicate ebb and flow design to balance. As such, seeking the balance from within is really what a 4 person should be attempting. Attempting to balance ourselves within the world around us is not really possible; however, maintaining stability within is one of the keys to life.
5 *ADAPTABILITY*	+ Humans have five senses ~ sight, sound, smell, taste and touch. We also have five fingers and toes. The number 5 is also linked to astronomy in that "[t]here are five Lagrangian points for the sun-Earth system and five different Lagrangian points for the Earth-moon system...,"[9] all of which relate to gravity. There is also the five-pointed star, symbolizing faith. Represents personal freedom, curiosity, change, versatility and transformation, giving those with the number 5 an adventurous spirit. It is *expansion* personified. They are masters at adaptation due to their openness to change, making those with this number extremely resilient. – Repetition is difficult. A lack of personal freedom can cause restlessness. There is also a specific and delicate balance for 5's in relation to partnerships. This is primarily due to their need for personal freedom, which requires a partner that respects their personal boundaries. Pride may also present itself in a negative manner.

[9] Specific quote obtained from: "https://bahaiteachings.org/spiritual-meaning-symbolism-significance-number-five" link.

#		DESCRIPTION
6 *STABILITY*	+	The sixth sense refers to Extra Sensory Perception (ESP), which is the cornerstone of the number 6. Six resonates with the planet Venus. Venus is representative of creativity and artistic abilities but also the union between partners. Represents love on all fronts, including unconditional love and, by extension, spiritual healing. Six people are nurturing and always of Service to Others. Ultimately, they are always attempting *"the greater good"* principles of humanitarianism. They provide protection, emotional healing and stability at the "community" level.
	–	Self sacrifice of both individual time and energy can present. Viewing life on a more "global," or "universal," level can make it difficult to concentrate on personal relationships and individualism. Remember to take time for you.
7 *SPIRITUALITY*	+	Seven is a very spiritual number, reflecting positive energy. Throughout several cultures on Earth, specifically during difficult times, there is a reference to "The Seven Sages." In Christianity, God completed the heavens and the Earth in six days, leaving Sunday as a day for rest. Seven represents intuition, wisdom, growing self-awareness and creativity. They are insightful, intellectual, introspective and exhibit wisdom beyond their years. As a result, they tend to pursue vocations relating to teaching and the healing arts.
	–	The shadow side of oneself is ever present. A delicate balancing act between darkness and light is the only way to achieve true peace. Although your destiny is to help others see their light, neglecting the shadow side of oneself will not complete the entire circle of understanding.
8 *TRANSFORMATION*	+	Eight represents infinity, the ebb and flow of time. Eight is also associated with abundance and prosperity, as well as rebirth, regeneration and transformation. Those born with 8 influences exude a sense of power and strength. They are efficient, disciplined individuals that exhibit a high sense of integrity and seek the truth in all things. They also have strong feminine energy.
	–	The number 8 is also associated with the planet Saturn. Saturn represents discipline to the extreme, which in turn can lead to rigidity. Having blinders, or being single minded, implies an inability to bend. As life is dynamic, ever changing, an inability to understand the fluidity of existence on Earth can be problematic. This can be avoided by looking at other points of view.

#	DESCRIPTION
9 *COMPLETION* + –	Nine is the number of completion and transformation, symbolizing power over a particular obstacle(s) that may have presented for several lifetimes. In other words, the finalization of a cycle or an alteration in consciousness. Number 9 is also associated with good fortune and prosperity, selflessness, humanitarianism, global awareness, versatility and spiritual awareness. Having a sense of "power" can always have negative connotations. If taken to the extreme those with the number 9 can present as aggressive and a bit opinionated. They are also known for being perfectionists.

The following chart represents the letters of the English alphabet with their corresponding numbers listed underneath.

ALPHA TO NUMERIC

1	2	3	4	5	6	7	8	9
A	B	C	D	E	F	G	H	I
J	K	L	M	N	O	P	Q	R
S	T	U	V	W	X	Y	Z	

Ex.3: Gary Gene Carter

7+1+9+7+7+5+5+5+3+1+9+2+5+9 = 75; 7+5 = 12; 1+2 = **3**

Numerology helps explain the archetypes presented for the human journey. Knowing, and being able to accept all aspects of personality, will provide a more straight forward understanding of self. The numbers reflected through one's name, as well as birth month, day and year, have significant influence on human behavior. "To know thyself" is incredibly important as one navigates his/her/their Earthly life.

As this is a "Beginners Guide," it is highly recommended that personal research continue. While there are several books on the market that provide an in depth look at numerology, an even more elevated comprehension of numbers can be found through the study of Sacred Geometry. Sacred Geometry relates to how specific geometric shapes and mathematical ratios are incorporated into the profound spiritual meaning of nature and the underlying structure of the universe. This topic will be explored in the book entitled "The Advanced Guide to Metaphysics."

Lastly, there are several disciplines that expand on the basics of numerology. The *Enneagram of Personality*, originally written by Oscar Ichazo (1931–2020), *The Human Design*, which was originally written by Alan Robert Krakower in 1992 and later revisited by Chetan Parkyn, and *The Gene Keys* by Richard Rudd, are all excellent books that will add to the understanding of the layers of an individual's personality.

CHAPTER 4

CHINESE ASTROLOGY

Chinese Astrology is an extension of Eastern philosophical thought. Like numerology, it has a single principle in mind. Chinese Astrology is based upon an annual calendar, as well as characteristics relating to the animal kingdom. Both Western and Eastern astrology base their information on the Milky Way constellations. Regardless of its origins, the purpose of Chinese Astrology is to assist humans in gaining a more compassionate viewpoint of their inherent essence, as well as that of others in their inner circle. It also provides a simpler understanding of personality types, allowing greater insight into human nature.

According to legend, as written by Theodore Lau, author of *Chinese Horoscopes Guide To Relationships*, Lord Buddha "...assigned a year to each of the twelve animals who came to bid him farewell on his departure from Earth" (p. 1). In ancient Chinese astrological lore, however, "...the study of horoscopes were based primarily on the theory of the Twelve Earth Branches governed by the twelve-year lunar cycle" (Lau, p. 1). Each corresponding animal is also noted to have an Earth branch, or Zodiac counterpart, which will be incorporated herein in the chart below. It is highly suggested that, once the Chinese sign has been researched and understood, one refer to its Western counterpart in Chapter 5, *The Zodiac*.

Each triad category: (1) Rat, Dragon, Monkey; (2) Ox, Snake, Dog; (3) Tiger, Horse, Rooster; and (4) Rabbit, Sheep, Pig; creates a special relationship known as the Triangles of Affinity. These composites of like energy create unity, much like the Zodiac signs that share the same elements in Western astrology. Other combinations can also be beneficial, while others may prove to be more challenging. "Relationships foster synergy and symbiotic bonds," a necessary element to leading a joyful existence (Lau, p. 5). Creating strong connections with others makes life easier and more worthwhile. The Chinese firmly believe that knowing which combinations work in tandem will ultimately bring about success in all forms of relationships. Those in the first triad are the *doers* within society. The second triad represent *thinkers*, the third triad *protectors* and the final triad are *catalysts*. This is the basic core of their persona, deeply embedded within their psyche from birth until death.

Chinese astrology considers one's year of birth as one's primary persona; however, time of birth, or the ascendant, is also factored when assessing one's true nature. If the ascendant sign falls under a stronger personality type than its primary, the latter can produce a more dominant representation. Lau states, "[o]ur ascendant's characteristics play a large role in our total makeup and may...not immediately be recognized in our personality" (p. 8). A fantastic example would be a rabbit/cat with a dragon ascendant. Think of the personification of the rabbit versus that of the dragon. Granted, the term "rabbit" is a bit of a misnomer as the Chinese did not domesticate rabbits until much later during their cultural history. Really, the true reference is The Year of the Hare. The Dragon, on the other hand, is rather self-explanatory. This resulted in the phrase "fire breathing bunny." Hopefully that particular analogy helps one understand how important an ascendant – time of one's birth, can be in one's chart. This particular topic becomes even more relevant in Western Astrology because it sets forth the placement of one's Houses with their planetary locations at birth being of the utmost importance. (See Chapter 5.)

The goal of every metaphysical *tool* is to help one achieve equilibrium. The current status of Earth, and its inhabitants, can appear rather chaotic. But the challenge is, at every point during humanity's evolution, to find peace wherever possible. Chaos, after all, is inevitable. The Third Dimensional Earth plane is built upon the principles of polarity, duality, cause and effect, spiritual growth and understanding. These positive and negative energies are constantly in motion like a wave, balancing back and forth until they level out and integrate. The achievement is a more peaceful existence. This occurs *only* through the process of evolution. The two steps forward and, hopefully, only one step back principle. That's progress! It should also be noted that humans are not meant to be alone. "When there is equilibrium or 'give and take,' in a relationship, we can truly say there is harmony" (Lau, p. 6). This requires interaction with one another.

The Chinese utilize a five element system, rather than a four (i.e., earth, air, fire and water). The element of "metal" has also been incorporated into their descriptions of each animal with a rotation that occurs in five year cycles. Every twelve years, the animal changes its element, which spans a sixty year time frame. Whatever element one's animal sign carries with it will add another layer to one's personality, as well as their reactions to circumstances.

Chart No. 4.1 indicates which hours apply to which animal with their corresponding element. It is highly recommended that each reader incorporate the time of birth into their overall understanding of not only their personality but of their significant others. The Earth element is added for even greater understanding with their true meaning provided in Chapter 5, *The Zodiac*.

Chart No. 4.1

ANIMAL	TIME OF BIRTH	ELEMENT
Rat	11:00 pm – 1:00 am	Fire
Ox	1:00 am – 3:00 am	Earth
Tiger	3:00 am – 5:00 am	Air
Rabbit	5:00 am – 7:00 am	Water
Dragon	7:00 am – 9:00 am	Fire
Snake	9:00 am – 11:00 am	Earth
Horse	11:00 am – 1:00 pm	Air
Sheep	1:00 pm – 3:00 pm	Water
Monkey	3:00 pm – 5:00 pm	Fire
Rooster	5:00 pm – 7:00 pm	Earth
Dog	7:00 pm – 9:00 pm	Air
Pig	9:00 pm – 11:00 pm	Water

Chart No. 4.2 provides detailed information concerning each animal represented in the Chinese Zodiac. The dates provided under each animal change every year. In other words, the year given may not be exact. For instance, a person born January 24, 1963, is still under the influence of the Tiger as, in that particular year, the year of the Rabbit did not begin until January 25, 1963, and ended on February 12, 1964. If born in late January to mid-February, it is best to verify the animal sign that accurately reflects the Chinese New Year calendar.

Chart No. 4.2

Name / Dates	DESCRIPTION
RAT 1924, 1936, 1948, 1960, 1972, 1984, 1996, 2008, 2020, 2032	As a *Doer*, Rats are hands-on people who love taking initiative. They are self-starters, positive thinkers, enthusiastic, capable, hard-working and fearless leaders. This first branch exhibits traits that include being "security-conscious, sentimental, thrifty and crafty" (Lau, p. 175). "More practical than emotional, more optimistic than wise" (p. 10). They are performance and progress oriented, as well as adept at handling matters through innovation. + Happiness comes to this triad through their ability to act on their ideas. *Pioneer *Negotiator *Instigator *Solver of Mysteries and Riddles *Charming *Articulate *Intuitive *Influential *Reveres Parents *Family Man *Industrious *Ardent *Good Judge of Character *Giving *Sentimental *Perceptive *Discerning *Speculative *Motivator *Sociable *Inquisitive *Excellent Communicator *Affectionate *Attentive
SAGITTARIUS –	*Outspoken *Opinionated *Competitive *Does Not Take Lightly to Defeat *Easily Agitated *Impatient *Petty *Manipulative *Schemer *Relentless Foe *Aggressive

Chart No. 4.2

Name / Dates	DESCRIPTION
OX 1925, 1937, 1949, 1961, 1973, 1985, + 1997, 2009, 2021, 2033 **CAPRICORN** –	As a *Thinker*, the Ox is pragmatic, rational, purposeful and reflective, valuing intellectual prowess and abstruse thinking. They exhibit superior intelligence and are the planners and schemers "...who plot the course for others to follow" within society (Lau, p. 10). They are also notably patient, thorough and steadfast with a perseverance that does not falter. They are considered the visionaries of society and have unwavering tenacity with a constancy of purpose. They follow their head, not their heart. *Enforcer *Methodical *Analytical *Strength through Unity *Exhibits High Levels of Perseverance *Patriotic *Hard-Working *Trustworthy *Logical *Great Stamina *Dedicated *Unpretentious *Honest *Traditionalist *Problem Solver *Sterling & Unblemished Reputation *Resilient *Dependable *Dedicated *Conscientious *Reliable *Practical *Industrious *Unyielding *Does Not Like Change *Strong Dislike of Failure *May Appear Unapproachable and Inflexible Due To Being the Strong, Silent Type *Not Receptive to New Ideas *Creature of Habit *"Stingy with Affection" (Lau, p. 56) *Unforgiving *Prideful *Stubborn
TIGER 1926, 1938, 1950, 1962, 1974, 1986, + 1998, 2010, 2022, 2034	As *Protectors*, Tigers are considered "Fiery, Emotional and Subjective" (Lau, p. 11). They are compassionate, selfless and of Service to Others who promote understanding and unity, oftentimes in an unorthodox fashion. This branch, however, also can be demanding, impulsive and impetuous at times, especially when their freedom is being thwarted. They are extroverts who are true to their individual beliefs, even if a bit emotional with a tendency toward being a tad bit volatile in temperament. It is part and parcel to their very passionate nature. They are, after all, *protectors*, which translates into advocates for the less fortunate. They can be loyal, sometimes to a fault with "...magnetic and [colorful] personalities" (p. 12). They are honorable with an innate sense of fair play. "Guided by their emotions, they can assess a situation accurately..." via their intuition and with nearly 100% accuracy (p. 12). These personality types are often found within the limelight of society, either on stage, in cinema or the political arena. *Idealist *Generous *Integrity *Colorful *Outspoken *Courageous *Humanitarian *Activist *Charming *Playful *Warm Hearted *Noble *Honorable *Honest *Intuitive *Magnetic *Optimist *Public Speaker *Excellent Sense of Humor *Innovative *Affectionate *Forthright *Decisive *Excellent Problem Solver

Chart No. 4.2

Name / Dates		DESCRIPTION
AQUARIUS	–	*Aggressive *Competitive *Dramatic *Defiant when Challenged *Rebellious *Obstinate when Working to Counteract Injustice *Commanding *Unpredictable *Suspicious *Undisciplined *Does Not Take Well to Criticism
RABBIT /CAT 1927, 1939, 1951, 1963, 1975, 1987, 1999, 2011, 2023, 2035	+	As *Catalysts*, Rabbits are highly intuitive, sympathetic and cooperative bringing "...about changes in others without changing themselves" (Lau, p. 13). They are supportive individuals in relation to the human condition. Sincere and generous, skilled at self-preservation but not as perceptive when it comes to other peoples motives, which makes them impressionable. This personality trait, however, also contributes to their artistic and creative abilities. They are "...experts in communication, computers, broadcasting, the movie industry..., and the world of music" (p. 13). They work behind the scenes, being the movers and shapers within society and prefer to stay out of the limelight. They "...have their fingers on the pulse of all segments of society and know how to make things happen for their own benefit, consciously or unconsciously" (p. 13). There intent is to bring about "...the universal spirit of cooperation" (p. 13), which can make them appear disloyal. In alchemy, a catalyst is described as "...something that causes activity between two or more persons or forces without itself being affected" (Dictionary.com). They bring about change, which is necessary for evolution. The "...Rabbit type's purpose in life is to maintain his own harmony and purpose" (p. 104).
PISCES	–	*Conformist *Arbitrator *Considerate *Approachable *Congenial *Astute *Obliging *Diplomatic *Intelligent *Prudent *Refined *Gifted with Gracious Manners *Self-Assured *Sophisticated *Keeps Thoughts to Self *Detests Gossip *Excellent Coping Mechanisms *Amiable *Sensitive *Wonderful Entertainer *Flawless Organizer *Thoughtful Friend *Private *Discrete * Ardent *Studious *Diligent *Chooses to Live an Uncomplicated Life *Aloof *Cunning *Detached *Insecure *Tendency to Rely on Others to Effect Necessary Changes *Vengeful *Ruthless *Calculating *Uncommunicative *Shrewd

Chart No. 4.2

Name / Dates	DESCRIPTION
DRAGON 1928, 1940, 1952, 1964, 1976, 1988, 2000, 2012, 2024, 2036 ARIES	As a *Doer*, Dragons are hands-on people who love taking initiative. They are self-starters, positive thinkers, enthusiastic, capable, hard-working and fearless leaders. This first branch exhibits traits that include being "security-conscious, sentimental, thrifty and crafty" (Lau, p. 175). "More practical than emotional, more optimistic than wise" (p. 10). They are performance and progress oriented, as well as adept at handling matters through **+** innovation. Happiness comes to this triad through their ability to act on their ideas. *Visionary *Benevolent Leader *Compassionate *Responsible *Idealistic *Optimistic *Energetic *High-Spirited *Honorable *Social Activist *Hard-Working *Dazzling Powers of Persuasion *Helpful *Forgiving *Ethical *Integrity *Honest *Non-Materialistic *Invaluable Fund Raiser *Magnetic *Fiercely Loyal *Protective *Excellent Public Speaker *Enthusiastic *High Strung *Opinionated *Competitive *Do Not Take **–** Lightly to Defeat *Demands Obedience & Loyalty *Dogmatic *Overconfident *Authoritative *Narrow Minded
SNAKE 1929, 1941, 1953, 1965, 1977, 1989, 2001, 2013, 2025, 2037 TAURUS	As *Thinkers*, the Snake is pragmatic, rational, purposeful and reflective, valuing intellectual prowess and abstruse thinking. They exhibit superior intelligence and are the planners and schemers "...who plot the course for others to follow" within society (Lau, p. 10). They are also notably patient, thorough and steadfast with a perseverance that does not falter. They are considered the visionaries of society and have unwavering tenacity **+** with a constancy of purpose. They follow their head, not their heart. *Strategist *Resolute Outlook *Sentimental *Introspective *Witty *Humorous *Artistic *Charming *Loves Beauty *Elegant *Reflective *Careful *Skillful Judge of Character *Studious *Observant *Focused *Good Business Acumen *Classical & Refined Tastes *Eloquent *Organized *Debonair *Analytical *Practical *Wise *Influential *Unyielding *Moody *Quietly Aggressive *Formidable *Does **–** Not Like Change *Strong Dislike of Failure *Secretive *Intensely Competitive *Vindictive *Possessive *Self-Centered

Chart No. 4.2

Name / Dates	DESCRIPTION
	As *Protectors*, the Horse personality is considered "Fiery, Emotional and Subjective" (Lau, p. 11). They are compassionate, selfless and of Service to Others who promote understanding and unity, oftentimes in an unorthodox fashion. This branch, however, also can be demanding, impulsive and impetuous at times, especially when their freedom is being thwarted. They are extroverts who are true to their individual beliefs, even if a little emotional with a tendency toward being a tad bit volatile in temperament. It is part and parcel to their very passionate nature. They are, after all, *protectors*, which translates into advocates for the less fortunate. They can be loyal, sometimes to a fault with "... magnetic and [colorful] personalities" (p. 12). They are honorable with an innate sense of fair play. "Guided by their emotions, they can assess a situation accurately..." via their intuition and with nearly 100% accuracy (p. 12). These personality types are often found within the limelight of society, either on stage, in cinema or the political arena.
HORSE 1930, 1942, 1954, 1966, + 1978, 1990, 2002, 2014, 2026, 2038	
	*Adventurer *Brilliant *Perceptive *Independent *Happy-Go-Lucky Attitude *Intuitive *Cheerful *Self-Confident *Brave *Bold *Self-Reliant *Vivacious *Most Adventurous of All 12 Signs *Requires Freedom *Good in a Crises *Agile *Forgiving *Spontaneous *Animated *Honest *Problem Solver *No Nonsense Approach to Life *Progressive *Proactive
GEMINI –	*Aggressive *Defiant when Challenged *Irreverent *Inconsiderate *Obstinate & Rash *Self-Centered *Fickle *Intimidating *Impatient *Vain *Restless

34

Chart No. 4.2

Name / Dates	DESCRIPTION
SHEEP 1931, 1943, 1955, 1967, 1979, 1991, + 2003, 2015, 2027, 2039	As *Catalysts*, Sheep are highly intuitive, sympathetic and cooperative, bringing "...about changes in others without changing themselves" (Lau, p. 13). They are supportive individuals in relation to the human condition. Sincere and generous, skilled at self-preservation but not as perceptive when it comes to other peoples motives, eluding to being impressionable. This personality trait also contributes to their artistic and creative abilities. They are "...experts in communication, computers, broadcasting, the movie industry...", and the world of music (Lau, p. 13). They work behind the scenes, being the movers and shapers within society and prefer to stay out of the limelight. They "...have their fingers on the pulse of all segments of society and know how to make things happen for their own benefit, consciously or unconsciously" (p. 13). There intent is to bring about "...the universal spirit of cooperation" (Lau, p. 13), which can make them appear disloyal. In alchemy, a catalyst is described as "...something that causes activity between two or more persons or forces without itself being affected" (Dictionary.com). They bring about change, which is necessary for evolution. *Peacemaker *Arbitrator *Approachable *Obliging *Diplomatic *Soft Spoken *Docile *Considerate *Compassionate *Unobtrusive *Talented *Artistic *Philanthropist *Charming *Excellent Powers of Persuasion *Acts with the Best of Intentions *Honorable *Forgiving *Nurturer * Versatile *Keen Observer *Debonair *Cultured *Respectable
CANCER –	*Sensitive to Change and Negative Energy *Insecure *Cautious *Overly Analytical *Masochistic *Argumentative *Procrastinator *Indulgent *Indecisive *Anxious

Chart No. 4.2

Name / Dates	DESCRIPTION
MONKEY 1932, 1944, 1956, 1968, 1980, 1992, 2004, 2016, 2028, 2040 LEO	As a *Doer*, Monkeys are hands-on people who love taking initiative. They are self-starters, positive thinkers, enthusiastic, capable, hard-working and fearless leaders. This first branch exhibits traits that include being "security-conscious, sentimental, thrifty and crafty" (Lau, p. 175). "More practical than emotional, more optimistic than wise" (p. 10). They are performance and progress oriented, as well as adept at handling matters through + innovation. Happiness comes to this triad through their ability to act on their ideas. *Innovator *Irrepressible Curiosity *Ingenious *Witty *Optimistic *Highly Intelligent *Inquisitive *Agile *Energetic *Resourceful *Objective *Spontaneous *Unconventional *Practical *Resolute *Excellent Judgment *Conversationalist *Astute *Diligent *Inventive *Sophisticated Personality *Magnetic Personality *Imaginative *Outspoken *Opinionated *Competitive *Do Not Take Lightly – to Defeat *Shrewd *Manipulative *Rebellious *Overbearing *Vengeful
ROOSTER 1933, 1945, 1957, 1969, 1981, 1993, 2005, 2017, 2029, 2041 VIRGO	As *Thinkers*, Rooster's are pragmatic, rational, purposeful and reflective, valuing intellectual prowess and abstruse thinking. They exhibit superior intelligence and are the planners and schemers "...who plot the course for others to follow" within society (Lau, p. 10). They are also notably patient, thorough and steadfast with a perseverance that does not falter. They are considered the visionaries of society and have unwavering tenacity + with a constancy of purpose. They follow their head, not their heart. *Administrator *Introvert *Efficient *Expert *Perfectionist *Diligent *Super-Conscientious *Meticulous *Extremely Organized *Dependable *Self-Sufficient *Fastidious *Sincere *Logical *Analytically Intelligent *Systematic *Observant *Chivalrous *Generous *Honest *Exemplary Researcher *Exhibit Great Amounts of Stamina *Civic-Minded *Hard-Working *Unyielding *Boastful *Formidable *Does Not Like Change – *Strong Dislike of Failure *Rigid *Nit Picky *Authoritarian *Tactless *Egocentric

Chart No. 4.2

Name / Dates		DESCRIPTION
DOG 1934, 1946, 1958, 1970, 1982, 1994, 2006, 2018, 2030, 2042	+	As *Protectors*, the Dog personality types are considered "Fiery, Emotional and Subjective" (Lau, p. 11). They are compassionate, selfless and of Service to Others who promote understanding and unity, oftentimes in an unorthodox fashion. This branch, however, also can be demanding, impulsive and impetuous at times, especially when their freedom is being thwarted. They are extroverts who are true to their individual beliefs, even if a bit emotional with a tendency toward being a tad bit volatile in temperament. It is part and parcel to their very passionate nature. They are, after all, *protectors*, which translates into advocates for the less fortunate. They can be loyal, sometimes to a fault with "... magnetic and [colorful] personalities" (p. 12). They are honorable with an innate sense of fair play. "Guided by their emotions, they can assess a situation accurately..." via their intuition and with nearly 100% accuracy (p. 12). These personality types are often found within the limelight of society, either on stage, in cinema or the political arena.
		*Guardian *Symbolizes Integrity *Loyalty *Traditionalist *Selfless *Thoughtful *Endearing *Truthful *Affable *Blessed with Stamina *Resilient *Charming *Modest *Peaceful *Altruistic *Honorable *Sensible *Brave *Rational *Possesses Unwavering Fealty *Team Player *Conscientious *Forgiving *Great Sense of Humor
LIBRA	–	*Aggressive *Defiant when Challenged *Impulsive *Rebellious *Restless *Guarded *Paranoid *Self-Righteous *Sharp, Sarcastic Tongue

Chart No. 4.2

Name / Dates	DESCRIPTION
PIG 1935, 1947, 1959, 1971, 1983, 1995, + 2007, 2019, 2031	As *Catalysts*, the Pig personality are highly intuitive, sympathetic and cooperative bringing "...about changes in others without changing themselves" (Lau, p. 13). They are supportive individuals in relation to the human condition. Sincere and generous, skilled at self-preservation but not as perceptive when it comes to other peoples motives, which makes them impressionable. This personality trait, however, also contributes to their artistic and creative abilities. They are "...experts in communication, computers, broadcasting, the movie industry..., and the world of music" (p. 13). They work behind the scenes, being the movers and shapers within society and prefer to stay out of the limelight. They "...have their fingers on the pulse of all segments of society and know how to make things happen for their own benefit, consciously or unconsciously" (p. 13). There intent is to bring about "...the universal spirit of cooperation" (p. 13), which can make them appear disloyal. In alchemy, a catalyst is described as "...something that causes activity between two or more persons or forces without itself being affected" (Dictionary.com). They bring about change, which is necessary for evolution.
	*Unifier *Generous *Arbitrator *Approachable *Obliging *Diplomatic *Honest *Chivalrous *Open-Minded *Jovial *Optimistic *Gregarious *Kind *Sensual *Team Player *Helpful *Lucky *Amorous *Relationship Oriented *Possesses Great Fortitude *Simple *Tolerant *Free of Pretense *Progressive Minded
SCORPIO	*Sensitive to Change and Negative Energy *Impractical *People – Pleaser *Insecure *Vengeful *Naive *Procrastinator *Difficulty with Being Objective in Matters of the Heart *Extravagant

Chinese Astrology is both fascinating and incredibly accurate with regard to personality traits. While it is often difficult to look in the mirror and face one's shadow side, it is also an opportunity to improve one's self by living on the positive side of the pendulum. It is highly recommended for those who have taken an interest in this Metaphysical approach to understanding the Universe to research their own animal, as well as those of friends, family and co-workers.

CHAPTER 5

THE ZODIAC

The Zodiac (Astrology) is at the core of human existence. Humans have reached for the stars since the beginning of time, even utilizing the constellations for navigation, plant propagation and harvesting of crops. The Zodiac embodies a wheel with twelve facets that ascend from their base above into a point that forms a triangle, all of which meet in the center. The Third Dimensional ("3D") world in which we exist is based upon matter, with the Fourth Dimension being the principles of time and space, or linear time with a past, a present and a future. As one travels through time and space in our 3D reality of matter, we experience only linear time, making the concept of an infinite existence difficult to grasp. This beautiful concentric circle represents a pattern that is dynamic and accessed with its variety of integration into every lifetime to provide a full spectrum of experience. Through this journey we come back to Source – the center of creation.

As stated in the prior chapter, Chinese Astrology is roughly based upon a yearly calendar. The Zodiac, also known as "Western Astrology," is based upon specific dates within a roughly 30-day pattern. It incorporates a variety of different modalities through angular aspects at varying degrees between two planets, which are known as Sextiles (60º), Squares (90º) and Trines (120º). This version will be extremely simplified; however, it will allow the imagination to sore and progress towards clarity of self, as well as others. It is highly recommended that *every* human have a Natal Chart completed by a trusted astrologer beginning in early adulthood. More specifically, between the ages of 18 and 21. Due to the complexity and amount of information divulged in a Natal Chart, revisiting is advised on an annual basis. One's birthday presents the perfect option. As planetary influences are constantly in motion, assessing potential shifts throughout one's life span is also advised, especially if concerned about a specific topic. Astrology offers a road-map to more optimistic opportunities, as well as potential blocks by offering a forecast concerning planetary influences that are in the moment.

I. THE ELEMENTS.

The first topic in astrology concerns the elements: Earth, Air, Fire and Water. Each of these elements are at the base of human development on Earth, and are the required substances for humans to remain its inhabitants. Earth is associated with carbon and minerals. Humans are carbon-based beings with internal organs and blood made up of the minerals from the Earth. Air with oxygen (all gases), fire with nitrogen and water with hydrogen. Earth has two essential parts. The first is a lower base that is *fixed* and immobile, and falls under the Zodiac signs of Taurus (earth), Leo (fire), Scorpio (water) and Aquarius (air) as one of their core qualities presents as stationary. The second is considered "rarefied, mobile and virtual" (Solaris – The 4 Elements of Nature as seen in her YouTube video *The Elemental Beings in Galactic History*), representing the physical aspect of Earth itself. Air is tangible atmosphere in the form of oxygen, all gases within the universe, as well as the intangible, volatile substratum, which refers to the spiritual aspect of human creation. The element of air is associated with the intellect, for which Gemini, Libra and Aquarius are influenced. Fire is associated with nitrogen, which is considered visible and invisible, discernible and indiscernible. Paracelsus describes fire as a spiritual, ethereal flame manifesting through a material, substantial flame. It ignites and propels humans toward something (a goal, a mission, etc.) Aries, Leo and Sagittarius are the Zodiac signs controlled by the element of fire. This particular element is an example of polarity, the true nature of the human experience. Water, associated with hydrogen, consists of dense amounts of fluid and exists in all Earthly creatures. Humans, and the Earth in which they all live, are made of roughly 80% of this particular substance. Cancer, Scorpio and Pisces are the triad linked to this element.

Elements work in tandem with one another in continual balance and expand the concept of polarity. The physicality of the Earth, and its mineral content, set forth the specific designated place with which homo-sapien, sapiens (a/k/a, "humans") exist in this 3D reality. The element of air, comprised of Nitrogen, Oxygen, water vapor, Argon and Carbon Dioxide, allows the body to sustain itself within the Earth's atmosphere. Through movement, air manipulates water by transporting it to and fro (i.e., via rain, hail and snow). Fire creates the warmth necessary for human survival during the winter months, as well as the ability to generate food sources.

In astrology, each element supports a specific type of energy but is also witnessed in Chinese Astrology, both of which add to its cadence. *Chart No. 5.1* provides the definition of each element and the specific type of magic it creates through its associations. These traits, along with their specific region within the Natal Chart, are at the core of one's approach to life.

Chart No. 5.1

Earth	The element of Earth concerns practicality, a sense of being grounded and stability. Their approach to life is presented in a pragmatic way by using logic, which creates a rather steadfast and true personality type. They are the signs of reliability and honesty. Earth signs also approach the sensual side of being human. When dealing with others, those with strong Earthly characteristics within their chart seek loyalty, security and predictability. Change is very difficult for those with heavy Earth influences. This requires a deep analysis of the exact location where Earthly influences fall within one's Natal Chart. The element of Earth is associated with the Root Chakra.
Air	The element of Air is associated with the intellect, innovation, communication, movement, freedom, liberation, creativity and truth. The Air element influences a deep desire for accuracy, which can lead to being a "perfectionist." This attitude plays out under the specific area of its planetary influences within the Natal Chart. Although perfectionism can have some rather negative connotations, it actually creates excellent critical thinkers, problem solvers and allows the ability to see the big picture. The element of Air is associated with the Heart Chakra.
Fire	The element of fire is transformative and regenerative. Its true nature is to "burn" away the old in order to make way for the new. Fire energy is dynamic and active, always in pursuit of variation. The negative aspects are reflected through destruction and chaos, for which is the result. From a spiritual standpoint, fire is a symbol of divinity, wisdom, knowledge and power. Those with fire in their Natal Chart are very passionate and creative but can also be authoritative. The element of Fire is associated with the Solar Plexis.

Chart No. 5.1

Water	The element of Water is associated with peace and wisdom that comes with age. It is the feminine, inward energy of reflection. Water epitomizes emotional depth, fluidity, purification, regeneration, fertility and cultivation. This particular element is a necessity on many levels. Blood consists of a certain percentage of water and is continually required in order to sustain human and animal life, as well as all the beauty present in nature. Approximately 71% of the Earth is covered in water (WorldAtlas.com), while the percentage of water within each human is approximately 60% for men and 55% (USGS.gov[10]) for women. Water, in the physical world, is fluid, thus causing movement in *all* directions. The element of Water is associated with the Sacral Chakra and the end of a cycle.

The next area of the Zodiac (a/k/a, "astrology") concerns the planets within the Milky Way Galaxy, specifically, our Solar System. Each planetary system, which includes the Sun and Earth's Moon, have distinct meaning, influences and purpose. When aspects are exhibited in a particular fashion [e.g., Moon Sextile (⁎) Mercury, Moon Square (□) Venus, etc.] there is a particular influence on the rise. Planets can also be "direct" or "prograde" which means moving in forward motion (West to East) or "retrograde" (East to West), which refers to moving "backwards," or in reverse as it is projected within the night sky from Earth's perspective. When there is a shift into a retrograde phase, many experience upheaval. All this really means is specific altercations, depending upon planetary influences, are inevitable. As humans have the blessing (and sometimes a curse) of *free will*, how one handles their choice(s) is paramount. According to Heather Roan Robbins, M.Th., retrogrades offer time to "[r]econsider, revise, repair and edit" past actions and "[a]ddress some unfinished personal business" (p. 46). Clearing out what no longer serves a purpose allows for an elevation in consciousness and, therefore, self expression. Additionally, each planet has its specific set of rules in relation to timing (number of days, months or years) as it orbits the Sun. When a planet moves from one astrological sign to another (e.g., Pisces to Aries, Leo to Virgo, etc.), a major energetic shift

---

[10] See article, *The Water in You: Water in the Human Body*, written by Water Science School, May 22, 2019.

is on the rise. How this affects the Natal Chart is an indicator of whether one perceives its influence as either "positive" or "negative." Sometimes, it is really just a matter of perspective!

The study of astrology begins with the Sun and the movement of other planets from one astrological sign to another. The Natal Chart shows where *all* the planets were at birth; however, planetary movement is dynamic. The Sun and the Moon are truly considered "luminaries," with their specific placements of the utmost importance. Each day has approximately twelve hours of day light and twelve hours of night (darkness), which is illustrated in the polarity of human existence. Both necessary; therefore, both of equal value. The cycle of the Sun begins on the spring solstice[11] with Aries, generally beginning March 21 through April 19, and ends with the sun in Pisces, the ending of the winter solstice. Robbins describes the significance of the Sun as "...the core of [one's] personality" and emblematic of the "... life force, ego, and consciousness" of every individual (p. 52) and rules the sign of Leo, the lion. The Moon denotes the emotional make-up of a person. Specifically, how one reacts to situations, usually of an emotional nature. It is also a reflection of how one nurtures others and the "how" of what is needed to be nurtured. Cycles of the Moon move relatively fast, at an approximate rate of every 27.5 days, changing signs roughly every two days and "...coloring our moods, habits, and behaviors" (Robbins, p. 54). The Moon is at home in the astrological sign of Cancer, the crab. Mercury is designated as the planet of communication and lightening quick action. Robbins indicates that it refers to one's "...mental switch-board: how you think, communicate, and move through the world" (p. 56). It travels around the Sun in approximately 58 Earth days; therefore, when viewing the Natal Chart it will usually be the same as one's Sun sign. Mercury is both the ruler of the air sign Gemini and the earth sign Virgo. Although this has been the standard for centuries, information gained over time leads to the possibility that Virgo is actually ruled by Maldek, the asteroid belt between Mars and Jupiter. That, however, is a topic for another day.

Before continuing with the descriptions of each of the planetary influences, there is another aspect to astrology that deals with one's energetic approach to life. They are referred to as "modalities" and there are three different types; Cardinal, Fixed and Mutable. The Cardinal signs

---

[11] Solstices deal with the in the length of time of night and day.

are consider the "alphas" within the astrological wheel. They have business acumen as they always finish what they have started, offering a fresh perspective. However, their negative polarity indicates a lack of stability and the need for balance. The Zodiac signs of Aires (fire), Cancer (water), Libra (air) and Capricorn (earth) exhibit independence, initiative, innovation, leadership and motivational qualities. Each of these Zodiac signs begins the initiation of Earth's seasons. The second aspect is reflected by the Fixed signs of Taurus (earth), Leo (fire), Scorpio (water) and Aquarius (air), which were briefly mentioned earlier. These personality types are considered reliable and persistent but also stubborn and immobile. The polarity to these more difficult traits concern the qualities of being steadfast, true and commitment oriented. They are also resolute, loyal, goal oriented, grounded, family-oriented individuals. The last of the modalities, refers to those who have *Mutable* characteristics, and concern the remainder of the Zodiac signs of Gemini (air), Virgo (earth), Sagittarius (fire) and Pisces (water). Their attributes relate to their versatility, flexibility, adaptable with the ability to see all sides of a situation, making them non-judgmental and even considered the wiser of the lot. Their less appealing nature relates to being flighty and highly impressionable. Each specific Zodiac sign has their own individual flair, adding a different flavor to each modality depending upon its association with one's Sun sign.

II. PLANETARY & OTHER INFLUENCES

A. *The Sun*.

The *Sun*, along with the Moon, are considered the greatest and most significant influences in one's Natal Chart. Their tandem luminescence is an essential factor to all living beings, including the plant and animal kingdoms. It's one's identity, self-expression and natural magnetism. The *Sun is* the center of our solar system, thereby holding the greatest magnitude of personal energy. The bodies physical attributes are also part and parcel to the effects of one's *Sun*, as each planet is ruled by a specific type of energy body wherein the *Sun* lies at the center. The solar plexus, or area of the upper abdomen of the body, is ruled by the *Sun* and, as stated in Chapter 1 on *Chakras*, refers to one's self confidence, self-esteem and stability without ego.

Sun energy is extremely powerful. It does, after all, light up our entire system of existence. It epitomizes personal power and vitality, creativity, clarity of purpose and authenticity. Where it lies within a chart is the beginning of one's understanding of themselves. It is also an opportunity to truly look at the polarity of one's nature. Where do the antagonistic aspects versus more harmonious attributes interfere with becoming a true reflection of one's authentic self? Finding the benefits to both is the logical answer. One must embrace all facets of who they are before truly understanding who they can then become. The journey to self discovery starts with the *Sun's* energetic influence.

Sun Association.

The sign of Leo is ruled by the *Sun* and, therefore, exalted for those born under its domain. Think about what that truly entails. The lion is proud, strong, fierce, courageous, beautiful, loyal and smart; therefore, those born under the sign of Leo are confident, generous, intelligent and indicate a larger than life personality. They are ruled by fire, which makes them warm, inviting and giving. They are also loyal to the core and self-assured, shining their light without any effort! The only real "difficulty" is found in relation to their fixed nature. Again, who is going to argue with the lion? False bravado does not truly exist with a Leo. Others may see it that way, however, their fixed sign creates an impermeable nature. The result is their steadfast and true, immovable loyalty. Can that result in negative consequences. Absolutely. The question, really, is "Where would humanity be if these characteristics were not prevalent within society?"

B. *The Moon.*

The *Moon* is illuminated by the *Sun's* energy and symbolic of one's emotional make-up and motivation but also includes a person's intuitive and nurturing capabilities. It also represents security and one's deepest needs. It is expression incarnate, revealing how one will react to any situation on an emotional scale. The *Moon* exhibits inspiration by stimulating creativity and imagination. Humans, regardless of their *Moon* placement, are ruled by their emotions. Sure, some are better at suppression than others; however, their reaction to the outside world will be one based upon their emotional conditioning and their *Moon's* location at the time of birth. The *Moon's* cyclical nature is approximately 27.5 days of rotation around the Earth, "coloring our moods, habits and behaviors" (Robbins, p. 54). During that time frame, it enters and exists every Sun sign until it repeats itself and the journey begins again. The good news is that a "moon effect" is short lived. It is the fastest moving "planet" in our solar system. This implies, on a short term level, that even if one is rattled by an emotional upheaval, which could stem from inside or outside influences, their ability to reign themselves back in rarely goes beyond a three day stent. Note here, the phrase "rarely goes beyond" has its own intuitive inference. One's ability to overcome their emotional "breakdown" is also dependent upon other planetary placements. More specifically one's *Moon* aspects and human imprinting[12].

The *Moon's* association is with the element of water and is ruled by the Fourth House of Home and Family. Robbins describes this influence as an emulation of "...early home life [that] impacts our sense of sanctuary and how we bring things to conclusion" (p. 100). The *Moon* has dominion over the tides within all ocean waters on Earth. The ebb and flow of all that is within the Earthly realm. An ocean can be calm and peaceful or stormy and unruly. It requires no provocation. According to National Geographic, ocean currents are controlled by "...wind, water density differences (due to temperature and salinity variations), and the Earth's rotation," which is referred to as the "Coriolis effect."[13] This effect is unpredictable and can not be controlled, only weathered. It is nature at its finest. The movement of the *Moon's* energy is cyclical, changing with the seasons. It's influence reaches far and wide. Its power lies within its control over Earthly existence.

Sun Association.

The *Moon* is ruled by Cancer, the crab. A crustacean that literally moves from side to side and never moves in a straight forward direction.

---

[12] Imprinting refers to "social conditioning." This is discussed in Chapter 8 entitled, *Michael.*

[13] See National Geographic article entitled "The Coriolis Effect: Earth's Rotation and Its Effect on Weather."

That implies a slight of hand with regard to how those under the spell of Cancer relate. It is really more of an analytical or intellectual reaction. Cancers are also Cardinal signs with excellent leadership qualities. Their ultimate goal is to provide a nurturing atmosphere but with strong and loving direction. They are extremely sensitive and deeply influenced by the tides of the ocean. It takes approximately one month to orbit Earth (approximately 27.3 days to complete a revolution, but 29.5 days from new moon to new moon)[14], moving through the constellations approximately every 2.5 days. This describes a constant shifting of the *Moon's* energy. Cancer's are also very intuitive and creative with a vivid imagination. Due to their receptivity to other people's energies, they need to remember to be a bit cautious when exposed to new people. Additionally, the astrological wheel shows that Cancer rules the fourth house of home and relationships, which includes pets. They revere their family and close friends, while absolutely adoring their animals of choice, considering them *all* a part of the family. The Fourth House is also associated with midnight, which some would claim as the magical bewitching hour when all things are possible!

C. *Mercury*.

Mercury emanates all forms of communication, adaptability and mental acuity. Communications are known to travel at lightening speed during specific Mercurial transits. When *Mercury* transits into a retrograde (see page 42) phase, batten down the hatches. Well, at the very least be prepared for several types of miscommunication, machinery repairs and, by all means, do not engage in any legal or business affairs. A formidable placing in the birth chart will help aid in one's ability to think fast on their feet and communicate in a way that is truly understood by the recipient. *Mercury* also concerns the sharing of ideas, which promotes a deeper meaning to life, often times, leading to heightened sense of self-knowledge. *Mercury* is known as the servant and the messenger of all other luminary and planetary influences, as well as *the* messenger of the gods.

---

[14] See "https://science.nasa.gov."

Sun Association.

Mercury rules both the signs of Gemini and Virgo. Its representation in Gemini, the twins, which expresses the duality of human's inherent nature, is associated with the element of air. Gemini also rules the Third House, which deals with early human development through education and childhood perceptions, as well as how one communicates and share's with others. It is also linked to short-distance travel and siblings. Gemini's are considered adaptable, witty, excellent communicators and storytellers, for which many are writers, even if unpublished. They are versatile, exhibit never ending curiosity with a highly intellectual and philosophical approach to life. Gemini's are also deeply intertwined with networking, which involves all types of social media. Their less than attractive characteristics are displayed through impulsivity, often leaping into situations before examining potential, sometimes resulting in dangerous outcomes. They also display a sense of insecurity; however, this is usually do to their sensitive nature and an unwillingness to cause harm to others.

Virgo's are considered more down to earth, methodical and forgiving, choosing to utilize their intellectual prowess in a more analytic manner but are less articulate then their air sign Gemini counterpart. Virgo energy is under Sixth House rule, running at the half way point through the Zodiac. This sixth House placements relates to all types of physical and mental health issues of well-being. The depiction of Virgo is the virgin woman/goddess holding a sheaf of wheat. This implies a deep connection to the harvesting of not only agricultural crops but that of relationships and work related projects. All of these concepts are enhanced by the Virgo principles of being meticulous, thinking before speaking and their flare for detail. They are also hardworking, dependable, organized, loyal, pragmatic and introspective. Virgo's are a reflection of the alchemist, wise teacher or sage, able to unfold transformation and transmutation. A Virgo's biggest downfall, for lack of a better word, concerns their judgmental and critical nature towards others. In part, these characteristics are representative of their more analytic approach to life and their own need to be perfect. And, if of any consolation, they are equally as demanding of themselves, often times more so than is truly understood. Either way, their characteristics are heavily linked to the world of communications.

D. *Venus.*

Venus epitomizes beauty, compassion, harmony, prosperity, abundance and pleasure, notably within the realm of art and music. She radiates mother-goddess, divine feminine energy and is never more than two astrological signs away from the Sun due to its jaunty rotation. Romantic connections, love and companionship are also an integral part of this planet's energy. *Venus* placement denotes how one views and accepts love in regards to all forms of relationships. This is the planet of generosity, charm, light-hardheartedness and joyful expression but through the reflection of personal values. Like Mercury, *Venus* can appear to rotate in a backwards motion (retrograde). Michael M. Meyer writes in his article, "Venus Morning Star – Venus Evening Star" (Astro.com), that *Venus* **exemplifies** emotional processes, attitudes and how one interprets, evaluates and makes sense of life-experiences." The "interpretations" of these individual experiences are, again, personal and have a direct correlation to the planet within which *Venus* falls within the Natal Chart and, of equal importance, its House[15] location. "*Venus* influences creativity and artistic endeavors" (Star, pg. 54), and symbolizes diplomacy, fairness and social graces. Those with a positive Natal Chart position are able to navigate social situations and cultivate meaningful connections with others but also within their community.

Sun Association.
Like Mercury, *Venus* rules two Zodiac signs; Taurus and Libra. While physical characteristics, such as a voluptuous body type, beautiful facial features and sensuality are congruent, the similarities between these two signs end there. Taurus has an earthy, fixed personality, while Libra is a Cardinal sign in the element of air. They both require solid relationships but have a very different approach, especially with regard to the way in

---

[15] House placements are determined by time of birth. It is a reflection of where the Ascendant was rising at the time and place of one's birth. If one is born at 7:20 am in San Diego, California, their Ascendant (or Rising) sign would be in Libra. As this is how the pattern of Houses are determined, the time of birth is crucial to a true Astrological analysis.

which they perceive them and their importance. Each of these individual signs approach partnerships very differently in order to achieve happiness.

Taurus is characterized by the bull, often referred to as "Ferdinand" and depicted in a field of beautiful flowers. *Venus*, as its ruler, implies that Ferdinand is peaceful, charming, enjoying himself in his blissful arena without a care in the world. While that may be true, the flip side to his happiness relates to any type of encroachment. Really, "Don't rain on my parade," or better yet, "Don't Tread on Me!," were probably written by someone born under a heavy Taurus influence. Most likely, their Sun or *Venus*. Taurus people are indeed compassionate, generous, love nature, are grounded, patient and loyal, with a love of the finer things in life. Their love of creature comforts is well known and can make them a bit materialistic. They have an earthy sensuality and sexual prowess. They are creative and artistic, which is usually connected with the earth in some way. "Cultivators" is an excellent word to describe them; whether is it through growing crops to share with others, tending to flowerbeds for the inherent beauty that is always provided, or sharing in the good life with family and friends. They relish fine dining or, at the very least, a variety of foods, especially sweets. What could go wrong, right? Think about the bull fighters of Spain. The lesson here is don't taunt the bull. Don't be waving a red flag in anticipation that Ferdinand will either appreciate or think it funny. To have aspects of one's nature under a fixed influence has a few real consequences. First, to put it mildly, it creates a personality trait of stubbornness. If pushed over the edge of reason, the Taurus is obstinate with an unwillingness to bend, making them an immovable force of nature. Attempting to control them feeds directly into their own need for control, especially in relation to assets and material worth, shared or otherwise. Sadly, this trait is not just in regards to situations but people as well. They also abhor outside interference to personal matters, which is understandable due to their grounded nature. The sign of Taurus falls under the Second House, which rules finances, material possessions, self-respect and boundaries.

Again, the Libran personality is also ruled by beautiful *Venus*. The energy of Libra, however, is presented in a leadership (cardinal), intellectual (air) format, yet it rules the Seventh House of relationships, mainly marriage and business partners. This can be rather confusing in relationships for both the Libra and their respective partner. The sign of Libra is the *only* inanimate object in the Zodiac. While this is helpful in a dispute, it is the opposite within an intimate relationship, which requires warmth and nurturing to survive. Libra is symbolized in the Major Arcana of the Tarot deck as blind justice, reflective of balance, equality, fairness and social justice. The primary goal is to be able to balance everything by weighing all the options through discernment, then by concluding which is the most viable solution. While for most it is easy to appreciate the ability to have equilibrium at one's fingertips, to the Libran it appears as a never ending circus, where being on a teeter-totter is the rhythm of the day. The key to survival for the Libran "on the fence" is to first find balance within his/her/them-self before they can "[l]ook at the whole situation for better composition [through] balanc[ing] the colors, the light, the shapes and the forms" (Robbins, p. 30), all of which will, eventually, lead to the best resolution. Another important factor, whether personal or in business, is to find an "equal" partner who can match the intellect and the beauty that life has to offer without compromising the Libran's core principles.

E. *Mars.*

Mars embodies the mythological god of war, the opposite of all that imbues the planet Venus. *Mars* combines all those traits of independence, aggression, as well as assertion, passion and strong will with single-minded action. It is motion incarnate but not necessarily with the wherewithal of grasping the consequences. Robbins refers to this energy as "raw" but believes this highly volatile energy has the potential to take flight toward a better day "...if you add wisdom and guidance" (p. 60). The *Mars* characteristics of bravery, strength, determination and protection are vital assets to humanity and are expressed through courage and honor. Those with enhanced aspects of *Mars* energy within their Natal Chart are those who fight for the underdog. They are the advocates of society and believe in helping those less fortunate.

Sun Association.

The First House of Aries, the ram, is ruled by *Mars*. Like the lion, consider the representation of the ram's inherent nature. Have you ever watched a ram in action? They butt each others heads to win favor in order to mate. They even stand on their hind legs thwarting their hooves at one another. It is the *Mars* energy of competition. They are the first sign of the Zodiac, making them independent, courageous and strong leaders, forging forth by igniting through initiative, imagination and innovation. For the Aries person, there is only winning that matters. Well, if they are a bit more mature, the flip side to that comment is the understanding that you can't win them all but, if you have given your best, that is what really matters. Those with Sun in Aires also exhibit qualities of honesty, optimism, passion and enthusiasm. Their power to combust can make them a bit overly ambitious, aggressive and impulsive but under their cardinal expression and fire energy, there is bound to be a bit of backlash. Without the pioneers of this world, there would be very little, if any, human progress. It takes the vision of the Aries person to venture forth and prosper. Through their pioneering ways, everyone benefits.

F. *Jupiter*.

This magnificent gas giant is approximately 2.5 times larger than any other planets within our solar system. Perhaps, that is why *Jupiter* is considered our greatest benefactor, and often times referred to as the planet of luck. Its bestows abundance, education, expansion, philosophy and travel. Some claim *Jupiter* energy also brings about wisdom. While this may be true, wisdom only materializes when one puts forth the effort. The very polarity of our existence requires expansion, recognition and knowledge of the spirit within before wisdom can manifest into reality. By experiencing all those trials and tribulations throughout one's lifetime, humans are rewarded if they are aware enough to see the relevance. How else are humans to learn if not by trial and error. Embrace this understanding rather than ignore it. The energies of *Jupiter*, specifically fortune and success, were specifically created to aid in one's ability to navigate through the world a little more easily. Setting forth one's intention, always in forward motion, is the key to obtaining all the many benefits *Jupiter* offers.

Sun Association.

Jupiter rules the Sun placement in Sagittarius, which provides the wonderful characteristics of an optimistic outlook on all life has to offer, even if under difficult circumstances found in early childhood. They are graced with immense curiosity that leads towards true spiritual evolution. They have a philosophical appeal, are forward thinkers, and focus on the expansion of consciousness through high ideals. They have a tendency to accept everyone as they *are*, without expectation, which aids in their mutable and friendly nature. Sagittarian influences everyone in some form, even if they don't land with any specific affiliation. The energy of Sagittarius still falls within every person's House placement, bestowing good fortune in at least one area of the Natal Chart. Like the attribute's found in relation to planet *Jupiter*, Sagittarian's are blessed with luck and good fortune. The have a philosophical approach to life, whether aware of it or not. They are adventurous and playful, independent and passionate like the other two fire signs; Aries and Leo. Their enthusiasm is contagious and accompanied by a friendly demeanor with a great sense of humor. They can present as a bit impulsive, impatient and reckless. They also tend to be blunt, which can come across to more sensitive types as a bit harsh or unfeeling. Yes, the truth often times hurts; however, sometimes it is necessary in order for a person to ignite.

G. *Saturn*.

Saturn embodies life, death and challenges but also rewards hard work. It is an elusive and powerful planet at the forefront of the lessons which are to be learned in this lifetime in order to move forward on an evolutionary scale. It lends a helping hand regarding the structure of humanity. Robbins has a great handle on *Saturn*, describing it relating to both personal authority, maturity, discipline, traditions and organization (p. 64). *Saturn* relates to the development or failure "...at taking responsibility, cultivating patience, perseverance, learning about the importance of structure, fair organization, higher order, prioritizing [and/or] completion of...goals" (Galactic Astrology 101 Course). Interestingly, *Saturn* in the Natal Chart can also affect how one approaches love and relationships. It takes approximately 29.5 years for *Saturn* to return to the same position it was in one's Natal Chart. It is known to have a profound affect, and with good reason. The point of laboratory Earth is spiritual growth, discovery and evolution, which is found through trial and error as one matures. Discipline and organization are required towards that end. If by the time one reaches roughly thirty years of age and they are not following the path of their initial intentions prior to birth, it is a wake up call, often with unpleasant consequences. Think of it as wisdom knocking at the door. Do you walk the path of wisdom or continue down the path of ignorance. Perhaps, even bordering on sheer stupidity. Ignorance is one thing, stupidity summons an entirely different meaning. With the first, one can cut themselves some slack; one can't know what they don't know. Stupidity means knowing and choosing to ignore the truth of a situation or circumstance. *Saturn* also signifies the end of the Earthly lessons and allows the outer planets of Neptune, Uranus and Pluto to work their magic in the spiritual realm of existence. If one can get passed all their past life lessons brought forth in this lifetime, the spiritual has a greater change of bringing the understanding of Source forward in positive motion. Let the fun times roll!

Sun Association.

Capricorn is ruled by *Saturn.* Like the ram, a Cardinal sign with excellent leadership skills, as expressed by the mountain goat that can climb higher than anyone would ever dream possible. Well, except the Capricorn, all of whom have no bounds. The sky is literally the limit, and they will keep rising until satisfied they have made it to the top. Actually, some just keep reaching for the stars, showing others that life is truly limitless. Materialization of the dream is actualized through determination, organization and discipline but within a healthy structure if the grand achievement is to crystallize. Capricorn energy relates to ambition, discipline, loyalty and determination but they can also be suspicious, pessimistic and critical. In mythology, Capricorn symbolizes a "mer-goat," which is half sea creature and half mountain goat. According to Robbins, mer-goat's are the representation of Spirit and the dream world (p. 64). This gives a more, well-rounded account of Capricorn energy. The Roman's believed *Saturn* was connected to the underworld and the Roman god of agriculture (Capricorn's are Earth signs) and time. Capricorn's are noted to be ambitious but hardworking, take a practical rather than fanciful look at life, and are very selective when it comes to their inner circle. This discernment with relationships is because they consider any "time" spent with others to be a tangible investment.

H. *Uranus.*

This planet is associated with change, or disruption, depending upon one's spiritual progress. The presence of *Uranus* in our solar system creates a willingness of humanity to assist with the greater good for all. It hones in on established structures, outdated modalities and even relationships that are without any growth and have become stagnant. It is known as the mover and shaker, creating chaos in its wake to bring about the necessary movement required on a spiritual and evolutionary level. Often times, *Uranus* forces the less than willing to look at their life and shift those old fashioned principles and values that no longer serve a purpose. *Uranus* energy is innovative but also unpredictable. It helps spur imagination and rules creativity and scientific genius. Humans tend to be habitual creatures. The role of *Uranus* is to upset the apple-cart, tip it over and leave the spillage to be cleaned up and reorganized. A bit scary, yes; however, it is also inevitable. Life is dynamic and all creatures, especially humans, must always be at the ready. Besides, what fun would there be in constant stagnation?

Sun Association.
Uranus rules the sign of Aquarius. This is a rather peculiar location. Aquarians are fixed, air signs. Seems a bit counter intuitive. How flexible is an Aquarian going to be with change when their sign is immovable? Aquarians are depicted as the water bearer. A person who fetches, carries and pours water, which makes them service to others oriented. *Uranus*, unlike *Saturn*, encourages freedom from tradition. Aquarians think outside the box and are innovative, philosophical and unconventional. Their greatest purpose is to "...weave people together to create community" (Robbins, p. 38). Through their beliefs and forward thinking, they are able to bring together a sense of unity consciousness. A task that is sincerely needed in the 21st Century.

I. *Neptune.*

The beautiful planet of *Neptune* consists of approximately 50,000 times more water than Earth, and was created to initiate humanity into spiritual transcendence through intuition and psychic abilities. It is concerned with the ethereal realms of existence, and deeply associated with enchantment. *Neptune* is the planet of inspiration, creativity, spirituality, and mysticism. *Neptune* is also responsible for humanities ability to imagine. It presents itself through ideas and artistic endeavors, usually through dreams and the subconscious. This is the planet of compassion for all things great and small, and involves the path of idealism. *Neptune* is also associated with the collective unconsciousness of humanity exhibited through the dissolution of boundaries and limits. It plays into one's hopes and fears, which can create illusions that surround both, making the future a bit blurred. The result is akin to a sense of overwhelming doubt, which can lead to addiction in order to escape the unknown. It asks questions; "Is this real or an illusion?" "How do I know the correct action necessary for the best outcome?" "How do I turn my dreams into reality?" All are accomplished by leaning into the divine spirit of Source and trusting one's intuition or gut reaction.

Sun Association.

Neptune rules Pisces, which is usually visualized as two fish swimming in opposite directions. Pisces are very emotionally sensitive, forgiving and highly intuitive, usually leaning toward clairsentience and/or clairempathy in relation to their clair gifts. (See Chapter 9, *Intuition*) Robbins describes their essence as "...a vast watery landscape with streams meandering over fields, through ponds and swamps, where the different elements and diverse species flow together in one subtle, boundaryless, and fertile landscape" (p. 40). That explains their rather dreamy and creative personality. They are romantic and extremely compassionate beings, making everyone they meet feel like a true friend. The more difficult task for the Pisces is remembering their own connectivity and sense of self. As a result, these particular types must always enlist healthy boundaries with whomever they meet. "Empathize with others but don't try to carry everyone else's pain for them and double the burden" is excellent advice (Robbins, p. 41). Pisces are the final mutable sign of the Zodiac, making their ebb and flow exalted in the element of water. This characteristic makes them adaptable in all matters; however, their sensitive soul also makes them vulnerable, especially to criticism.

J. *Pluto*.

This planet deals with the depths of the soul's evolutionary existence. *Pluto* is known to rule the underworld, which really is a reference to the shadow side of one's personality. It takes 248 years for *Pluto* to orbit the Sun; therefore, it takes its time to reveal the real magic it bestows. *Pluto* requires a deep dive into one's self. Going inward to redeem the negative aspects in order to come out the other side with a greater understanding and sense of purpose. This type of growth cannot be obtained without taking stalk of one's behaviors and reactions to both positive and negative aspects of self. The end result is transformation, not only of one's current human existence, but on a deeply spiritual level. An elevation, if you will, toward the unification of all that exists. Going beyond the ego with a heightened sense of awareness. This creates a bit of magic, which must be used wisely and not for personal gain. In a way, it is like finding buried treasure. This planet does not, even remotely, offer the easy path toward self-discovery. Nothing ventured, nothing gained. *Pluto* is a reminder to let go of the past, as it serves no real purpose except to hold one back from the realization of all their potential and spiritual enlightenment. The inner work of *Pluto* brings forth what is necessary for personal improvement and the evolution of one's consciousness.

Sun Association.

The association of *Pluto* is connected to the deeply misunderstood sign of Scorpio. Many moons ago while studying Western Astrology, an interesting facet of this sign was uncovered. From an evolutionary perspective the sign of Scorpio is split into three spiritual pathways: (1) Grey Lizard; (2) Scorpio; and (3) Eagle. Basically, this sign is split into three levels of cosmic understanding. One could say that it is broken down into the soul's spiritual journey by way of how far that person has traveled toward becoming one with Source. The Grey Lizard represents the beginning of that souls cycle. Perhaps, the "Baby" or "Infant" soul. These terms are described in more detail in Chapter 8, and are akin to the growth of the human being and what is obtained from birth to the age of 10. The Scorpio is the "Young" and "Mature" soul, also discussed in Chapter 8, affiliated with the ages of teenager to adulthood, ages 11-35. The "Old" soul is adulthood until death. Scorpions, the mid-range of age for Earthlings, is what is primarily considered here. Scorpio's are passionate, brave, resourceful, sexual, curious and observant. These traits relate to every life stage of this sun sign. The more evolved Scorpio, including the Eagle, are exponentially more intuitive, loyal, analytical and transformative. Negative aspects for all types include being judgmental, secretive, stubborn and jealous. Robbins describes the symbols of Scorpio and Eagle with differentiating perspectives. The Scorpio has the "...ability to burrow under the rocks of the psyche or culture," which appears to make them secretive; however, it is also a testament to their need to uncover the truth of a matter without snap judgments (Robbins, p. 32). The Eagle "...invokes both the soaring heights of the eagle's perspective...", and that of the Scorpio simultaneously (Robbins, p. 32). There is a certain mystery to all levels of Scorpio. Although once believed to be ruled by Mars and *Pluto*, the later has a greater association because the end game of the Scorpions nature is to get to the bottom of a matter to evoke personal and spiritual growth. This requires a great amount of investigative observation, patience and understanding.

CHAPTER 6

CARTOMANCY

Cartomancy, which is also referred to as "divination," relates to the use a deck of cards to determine one's opportunities, obstacles and potential course, or courses, of action. Although Wikipedia claims that Tarot cards came after the standard 52-card deck, this is inaccurate information. The use of Tarot cards dates back, at the very least, to Atlantian times, approximately 11,500 years ago. Perhaps even longer. The author is not alone concerning the actual timing of this ancient source of wisdom. In the book, "Spiritus Mundi," written by Elizabeth Kim, she corroborates the above via information obtained in her research. Antoine Court de Gébelin, an 18th Century Freemason, claimed in 1781 that "...the tarot was actually an ancient system derived by the occult knowledge of Ancient Egyptian priests" (Kim, p. 87). William Henry, an extinguished writer and speaker in relation to humankind and our ascension from the Third Dimensional realm to the Fifth, would agree with Kim's assessment. Many authors and researchers concerning the knowledge of ancient civilizations have recently determined that Atlantis and Egyptian cultures were extant on the Earth simultaneously. For the purposes of this *Beginner's Guide*, the focus here will be on a much smaller scale that does not include Tarot card information, with exception of Chapter 7, which covers the archetypes of the 22 Major Arcana. There are several different types of decks with which to choose and they are an excellent tool for increasing one's intuitive abilities. According to "guardian.co.uk," the Chinese invented playing cards before 1,000 BCE.[16] The standard playing card deck of today, however,

---

[16] "BCE" refers to "Before Common Era," formerly known as "AD," "After Death," denoting the former Christian reference.

was created sometime during the 11th Century. Although considered a bit archaic in today's modern age, a basic standard deck of cards is still used to gain better insight into circumstances that vex the human condition. This *Beginner's Guide* will cover a few types of cartomancy decks: Oracle/ Divination, Russian Gypsy Cards, and those representative of the ancient Chinese fortune-telling "game" known as "Gong Hee Fot Choy."

I. ORACLE CARDS.

In many ways, oracle cards are different from other forms of cartomancy. Each oracle deck resonates to a specific category or theme, and offers problem solving solutions along with foresight on a wide variety of human related topics. According to goddesselite.com, "Oracle decks offer guidance, clarity into a situation and even new perspective." Oracle cards are also an easy way for an individual to concentrate on a singular message while conducting meditation or connecting to Source or Spirit Guides. A question is asked, a card is drawn (perhaps daily, bi-weekly, weekly, etc.), the information ascertained. It is highly recommended that, at a minimum, a brief meditation follow to help one better comprehend the course of action required for a positive outcome. Daily affirmations for spiritual growth and creating oneness with Source are also a fantastic way to start and/or end the day, as well as a way to assist with gaining vital knowledge about oneself and our universe.

A. *Fairy Wisdom Oracle Deck:*

According to authors and creators of this particular deck, Nancy Brown, writer and metaphysical healer, along with her daughter, the artist Amy Brown, the spiritual realm is inhabited by charming fairies, angels, dragons, elves and other elemental guides that are willing and able to assist with our spiritual development, while creating a safe space for learning. The author of these cards believe fairies provide a bridge to the elemental/ realms. Fairies always have one's best interests at heart, which is why they created the stunningly beautifully deluxe set of 64 cards and 140-page illustrated book. The cards, along with its book, incorporate wise messages from fairies, along with chants to help you focus your intentions and embrace a more positive attitude toward life. "We do not live independent of one another but are interdependent…" and "[t]hese wonderful beings are here to help" on our journey toward a greater understanding of our human existence (p. 3).

Each card within this particular deck depicts a "keyword" insight into any question asked. This is an incredible helpful beginner's deck, as it allows one-word readings without the complexity of symbolism. The types of spreads suggested can glean a wide range of information, depending upon the recipients wishes. This oracle deck is simply delightful fun with the ability to bestow brilliant and wise knowledge, enhancing each recipient's spiritual development.

B. *Mystical Healing Reading Cards*:

These divination cards were created by Inna Segal to facilitate the awakening of one's "Spiritual Self." She explains in her Introduction that everyone needs "…access to a greater wisdom, which lives inside [one's] heart and soul[,] as well as in the Higher Dimensions of existence" (Segal, p. 1). They are thought provoking and beautifully illustrated by Jake Badderley, whose art depicts mysticism incorporated with ornate symbolism. The most fascinating parts are the 36 options available, each of which contain a course of action to promote and guide one toward success and fulfillment. They include, but are not limited to, modern day themes in relation to one's own emotional state of awareness. Segal explains that by exploring one's feelings around important, relevant, personal issues relating to "… fear, anger, criticism, guilt, control…", and the like, the development of objective thinking becomes possible (p. 2). Ultimately, by working through negative, shadow energy you are able to reach "…your highest truth" (p. 2). The primary goal for Segal is to help those who participate "…in a more meaningful way to live" (p. 2). Is that not the point of this life's journey?

On a personal note, use of this particular deck has had significant effects, both individually and professionally by way of providing transformation for those seeking clarity of action in their lives. They break down complicated issues by simplifying information that allows one to get to the point of the issue at hand. Excellent for those seeking a daily affirmation to start their day.

II. DIVINATION CARDS.

A. *Galactic Heritage Cards*:

Created by Lyssa Royal-Holt (hereinafter, "Holt") in 2013, the Galactic Heritage Cards remain the first and only of their kind. They are based upon Royal-Holt's book, "The Prism of Lyra." The specifically designed 108-card divination system, which was created to help individuals embrace their star lineage and karmic patterns, goes far beyond just extraterrestrial knowledge with divine wisdom. Galactic Heritage Cards reveal individual lessons brought to Earth from other star systems that can enhance one's Earthly and spiritual journey. Additionally, utilizing these cards provides the opportunity to discover both past life incarnations and current karmic lessons. All of which will allow the necessary shadow work to be completed in order to find one's light.

B. *Russian Gypsy Fortune Telling Cards*:

Russian Gypsy Fortune Telling Cards (hereinafter, "Russian Gypsy Cards") have a mystical power that predicts both favorable and unfavorable life circumstances and events. Their origin dates back to sometime during the early to mid 18th Century, and they are derived from aspects of Russian Folklore. During the week, "[p]eople wanted to have their fortunes told because it was a time they could concentrate on themselves, talk about their feelings or frustrations, and formulate strategies for the future," while Sundays were reserved for worship (Touchkoff, p. 3). Svetlana Alexandrovna Touchkoff, the originator of this particular deck, states the cards are akin to "...*a psychic barometer*..." that alerts one to their *current* vibrational energy (pp. 3-4). The cards are also a reminder of the cyclical nature of the universe (i.e., birth, death, the seasonal nature of Mother Earth, etc.), making them extremely beneficial. They provide clarity, thereby allowing one to see a situation (or situations) from a different perspective (or perspectives). The most important notation made by Touchkoff is that "...the cards do not seek to control us..." because "[h]ow we see events and react to them is left to our own free will" (p.4). Again, *discernment* being the key factor. Russian Gypsy Cards are a fantastic personal problem solving tool that ultimately leads one toward the "common good" or favorable solutions and universal standing by utilizing "synergistic energy," which is a combination of "...conscious and unconscious thoughts to make a stronger whole" (p. 6).

This cartomancy deck is made up of 25 beautifully designed square cards measuring 4" by 4" in diameter. As they are not as ancient as Tarot cards, they relate to more modern day affairs and concerns, which includes Christ consciousness and the divine light that purports the Christian faith. Each card contains four triangular pictures with four corresponding arrows showing its intended direction (↑, ↓, →, ←), and are laid out five cards in each row, with a total of five rows. There are four potential variations to each card, giving this particular deck a total of 200 possible responses. Each full picture has an initial connotation that is enhanced by the direction of the arrow. The book that accompanies the deck is replete with details and provides the story behind its creation, as well as the author's personal knowledge past down through generations.

C. *Gong Hee Fot Choy*

The English translation of this cartomancy "game" translates as "Greetings of Riches." While it is advertised as a "game," it is a form of divination, and based upon both Chinese astrology and numerology. According to Margarete Ward, numerologically speaking, this form of divination confirms the ancient belief that "...life's odds are three to one in favor of good over evil" (back page), including prosperity over poverty, success over failure, and good fortune over bad. It is also thought that the future can be forecast, even influenced, if we know how to interpret the signs and their often symbolic meanings. The foregoing also relates to the number "3" discussed in Chapter 3 on *Numerology*.

The spread is singular in nature and uses a portion of a standard deck of cards. All number two's through sixes, as well as the Joker are eliminated, leaving the remaining 32 cards of the standard deck to be used. Additionally, each suit has a specific energy of resonance. If certain suits are lined up in a specific way on the sheet that is provided, or specific numbers fall into sequencing, it gives a deeper meaning to the reading.

Before concluding this chapter is should be noted that insight is not actually in the cards. "Cards are just a mirror that focus your inner energy and reflect an aspect of yourself so you can see it clearly" (Holt, p. 31). In Lyssa Royal-Holt's *Card Meanings and Commentaries* inserted into her *Galactic Heritage Cards*, she adds "[a]ll card systems require truthful self-observation without judgment" (p. 31). This should be a mainstay and remain present during all readings, whether reading for oneself or for others. The information gained while reading is astounding, even if the accuracy is not one hundred percent. As a matter of course, no Intuitive or Psyche person can predict future events with that kind of accuracy. Earth life is dynamic, every changing with each choice one makes. What is stated during a session is, in essence, more validation than prediction. Cartomancy is tapping into your personal energy field, Higher Self and the Divine. A source of information that one always has available but may be leery of believing. That is why no card reader or specific deck with which is chosen to read is ever the same. For every Tarot card, or other form of Cartomancy, reading that has been given over the past 35 years, not one "reader" has interpreted the cards in like manner. *Always* keep in mind that you are the captain of your ship. Your decisions are exactly that, *your decisions*. While it might be fanciful to think otherwise or blame others for a poor decision, you are responsible for the effect (what occurs thereafter) of your cause (choice).

CHAPTER 7

MAJOR ARCANA

The Major Arcana of every traditional Tarot card deck represents one's life lessons, which can include karmic debts, and the archetypal themes of the human experience. The initial design of any deck has a plethora of deep symbolism and esoteric information to help the interpreter relay the pertinent information during a reading to its recipient, referred to as the "Querent." This chapter will provide clarification of the traditional meanings behind the intention of each of the twenty-two Major Arcana cards, which are also equated to *The Hero's Journey*. It takes effort to transform oneself. The Fool's progression toward spiritual evolution should occur for each and every human several times during each lifetime on Earth. The Tarot is indicative of the subconscious mind, which is why choosing to have a seasoned reader can be an effective learning tool. The purpose of this exercise is to help one open their mind to the symbolism that surrounds everyone on a daily basis through our spiritual connection with Source. Often times, "synchronicity" is the way in which such information is conveyed. While the Tarot purports to encompass the "material" world on Earth, the actual point of the Fool's journey is to reach a destination that promotes spiritual awakening.

Even deeper still, Quantum Physicist Dr. Theresa Bullard-Whyke, equates human evolution beyond the normal Earth based comprehension, believing that the esoteric meaning of the Major Arcana reaches far beyond Earth into our entire solar system, and teaches about the 22 significant planets within the Milky Way Galaxy that are accessible to human consciousness. Something never taught in any book concerning the principles of the Tarot.[17] It should also be noted that the corresponding number associated with each Tarot card links to its numerological counterpart, all of which has been discussed in Chapter 3, as well as this solar systems planetary influences and astrological connections discussed in Chapter 5. The utilization of the Rider-Waite deck is where the explanations below have been explored.

I. Fool.

The Fool (a/k/a the "Neophyte") begins unnumbered at "0," signifying the very beginning of the souls journey toward self-discovery, which requires a leap of faith. The Fool represents the empty-set, nothing or void of the zero quantum field of existence. He is shown as a non-gender youth holding onto a knapsack or "satchel," getting ready to step off into the unknown with his trusty, loyal dog of the animal kingdom. He is full of glee as he awaits the wisdom of his journey to be revealed. He has magical items with him as well; all of which will help him on his mission toward self-awareness. He has a hat with a feather, representative of the animal kingdom but also the element of air. A white rose, associated with the plant kingdom. The satchel keeps his stored memories, or "child-like wisdom"[18] with which he can rely upon when necessary.

The Fool begins, again, on a new journey toward the unknown with the hope of self-discovery, and a greater understanding of the purpose of his existence. If this card is drawn, it is the ending of what was no longer serving a purpose and encourages the Querent to move boldly into the unknown. The Fool is connected to the planet Uranus, which influences a childlike innocence as one moves forward toward their latest and greatest quest.

II. Magician.

The Magician is numbered "1." He is considered the divine masculine aspect of creation. As the Fool begins his journey, how will he forge his

---

[17] At least any book by the author over the past 61 years!
[18] Quote from "Mystery Teachings" on Gaia TV by Dr. Theresa Bullard; Season 4, Episode 1, dated November 1, 2020.

desires? His right hand points to toward the sky with a double-ended wand, a symbol of his ability to channel energy and act as a conduit between the physical and spiritual realms. The bright yellow light that surrounds his entire body represents "...the element of air and his radiant light of the spirit..."[19], the white light connotes he is surrounded by divine energy. He brings together his creative ideas with the ability to make them come to fruition, even amongst chaos. His left hand points toward Gaia, implying the necessity of taking action toward that which one wishes to manifest. Together, the right and left hands serve as the concept of "as above, so below," derived from the "Emerald Tablet of Hermes Trismegistus," an ancient Hermetic text. This principle brings forth the understanding that the patterns observed in the celestial realm are also mirrored reflections of the earthly realm. The unification of All That Is. The infinity sign above his head is a reflection of the universal understanding that humans are eternal. On the table in front of him lie the four elements of air (sword), fire (wand), challis or cup (water) and pentacle (earth), all of which are symbolic of the earthly tools at his disposal. The foliage of greenery, Rose of Sharon and Lily of the Valley are displays of his ability to cultivate all his desires, which always requires attention, just as a garden always needs tending. His white robe of purity and his red robe of knowledge and experience along with his active use of will prove he is worthy. Remember, life takes effort. This is how success is often measured.

If this card is drawn, it implies one must embrace their creative energy and set forth their intentions by making a concrete plan toward that end. The time is *now*. The Magician is connected to the planet Mercury, which is linked to communications, networking, travel and creativity. These are the tools at one's disposal and should be utilized on *The Hero's Journey*.

III. High Priestess.

The High Priestess is represented by the number "2," and reveals the polarity and duality of this Earthly existence. She is the sacred, divine feminine aspect of creation. The Yin to the Magician's Yang. Her white

---

[19] Quote from "Mystery Teachings" on Gaia TV by Dr. Theresa Bullard; Season 4, Episode 3, dated December 1, 2020.

robe is purity, while the blue evokes celestial wisdom and power but shown to be flowing; a product of vibration or movement. The diadem above her head shows her Goddess prowess, linked to Isis (Egypt) and Hathor (Venus & Hadar), while behind her are pomegranates, illustrating her sexuality. The cross symbolizes the "as above, so below" principle of correspondence. She sits quietly in the temple on her cubical stone, an imitation of her soul, between two pillars of Solomon's temple, the presence of God ("J"), and His strength and omnipotence ("B"). It is time to reflect, contemplate and meditate before manifesting the seeds of the Magician. The High Priestess is our subconscious mind, offering the highest source of wisdom. She is a reminder to trust our inner knowing and to access the knowledge that lies deep within our subconscious mind.

The High Priestess embodies the constant flow of energy. If this card is drawn, it is to inform the Querent not only to trust gut reactions and intuition, but to also gain understanding regarding the polarity that is ever present on Earth. The High Priestess is connected to the Moon, the intuitive and nurturing side of human nature. She carries the power within to make the Magician's wishes ("seeds") come true.

IV. Empress.

The Empress is linked with the number "3," wherein the Magician and High Priestess have come together to create offspring. She is the "Mother" archetype and represents fertility, nurturing, creativity and abundance, as well as the start of a new business venture. She sits on a thrown, indicative of her "Queen" status, holding a scepter, which relates to the power she wields over her dominion. She wears a crown of twelve stars, a connection to the constellations within the Milky Way Galaxy, and an indication of her relationship with the Zodiac. There is wheat at her feet, showing her dominion over agriculture and all the Earth has to offer in abundance. Nurturing is her forte and depicts the clear understanding that in order for one's desires to be manifested, they must always be cultivate until they can bear fruit.

The Empress is associated with the constellation of Taurus and the planet Venus, as portrayed on her heart-shaped shield placed at the right side of her thrown. The trees in the background, and wheat at her feet, delineates her connection to the element of Earth, which emphasizes her grounding, life-giving qualities. When this Tarot card presents, it is conveying to the Querent the need to be patient while the Universe provides the magic that is required to cultivate all possibilities required for wish fulfillment.

V. Emperor.

The number "4" presents as the Emperor in the Tarot. He is the "Father" archetype, epitomizing authority, courage, intelligence, leadership, power and responsibility. He too sits upon a throw in a barren mountain landscape, emblematic of his ability to manifest that which he desires through "sterility of regulation and unyielding power." His thrown depicts the head of a ram in four locations, and he holds tightly to his Ankh scepter and a golden globe in his left hand, an implication of the magnitude of his presence. His red robe is a reminder of the power he bestows within his community. He is also involved in the building of structures, both physical and those relating to the business world.

The Emperor is associated with Aries, the ram, and the first sign of the Zodiac. When this card appears in a reading it implies that the Querent is in control of his/her/their life. Pay attention to the location within the spread as this is the true indicator of where the "control" or power is emphasized. The use of Assertion is warranted, not aggression. Be mindful of the difference.

VI. Hierophant.

The Hierophant (a/k/a, The Pope or The High Priest) is connected to the number "5." He is a devoted spiritual leader, priest, preacher or mentor who offers guidance to those within his community, and possibly beyond. His right hand is raised, representing benediction, with two fingers pointing skyward and two pointing down, forming a bridge between Heaven and Hell. Again, the "as above, so below" principle. The left hand holds a triple cross, while the crown atop his head has three nails protruding from it, symbolic of the crucifixion of Jesus. He is dressed in papal robes of red, referencing his gifts of knowledge and experience, creating a bases for others to feel comfortable in his presence and deem him trustworthy of their secrets. The keys siting upon his lap signify his authority and access to spiritual knowledge. The two pillars impersonate his strong foundation, which has been built upon the concept of the holy trinity. The pillars also symbolize law (obedience) and freedom (disobedience). He exemplifies cultural traditions and established values, which implies his deep need to keep social order and maintain the status quo. He is also known as the "reveler of secrets," which implies his abilities to impart divine wisdom. As one matures, the Hierophant offers guidance to those who seek the path toward enlightenment.

The Hierophant is linked with the planet Jupiter, which grants inspiration and imagination to the Querent. Jupiter is the planet of expansion, good fortune, luck and personal expansion, which can only be obtained through the gaining of knowledge brought about by discipline and hard work. When this archetype presents, there should be a sigh of relief, for the path toward self-awareness has been actualized. It is also a sign to continue with the expansion of one's consciousness through study. The goal, or one's desires, have yet to be reached, and while this is a reprieve of sorts, it doesn't convey that one should rest upon their laurels. Instead, trust the wisdom that has been afforded.

VII. The Lovers.

The number "6" in the Tarot are The Lovers. As much as the Lovers infer the archetype of union, commitment and relationships inherent in the human experience, the deeper meaning is meant to reference one's choices. Choices in all matters, not just those of the heart. Although the masculine and feminine appear in this card, they are the energies of Masculine, Father God and Divine energy, as well as that of the Feminine, Mother Goddess and Divine energy, not actual "gender." The Lovers card denotes love, deep connections and harmony through vulnerability in all types of relationships. More importantly, it symbolizes self-discovery, as well as growth by staying grounded and being true to oneself regardless of outside influences. As one walks the journey toward self awareness, outside sources will attempt to intervene through their own restrictions placed by the imprinting of both parents and social mores. This card informs and warns the Querent to stick to their own path. The Rider–Waite version of the Lovers card includes the tree of the knowledge of good and evil with a serpent wrapped around its trunk. Perhaps a symbolic warning of temptation.

The Lovers are affiliated with the Zodiac sign of Gemini. Here, the Querent must learn to make difficult decisions, which require discernment. The decision may require sacrificing a specific aspect on his/her/their part. Is the sacrifice worthwhile is the question.

VIII. The Chariot.

The Chariot connects to number "7." Although the figure at the helm appears male, there is no gender association. There are no ropes controlling the sphinxes (or horses), one black and one white, that are propelling the Chariot forward. The mallet on the front of the chariot is a masonic symbol that embodies self-control. In the Rider–Waite Tarot deck, the figure bestows a crown with a star atop the head, as well as stars on his canopy and "outfit," which implies celestial influences are present. The fact that there is nothing driving the sphinxes hints at the idea that the figure has utter faith as he/she/they will move forward toward their desires.

The Chariot is the personification of willpower, which promotes victory and a favorable outcome. The conflicts that may have come into play due to making difficult decisions has taken a turn for the best, most positive outcome. The Querent shows success through decisiveness by focusing on discernment. By weighing all consequences, and through hard work and commitment, he/she/they have forged a new, more valuable solution toward their ultimate goal that began when he/she/they stepped off the precipice as the Fool, welcoming the challenges that lie ahead.

IX. Strength.

Strength corresponds to the number "8." Depicted by a beautiful young maiden clasping the lion's mouth, signifying the ultimate capabilities and triumph over major obstacles that have been present over the course of the Fool's journey. She wears white, which stands for purity with flowers adorning her gown and her crown. Above her sits the infinity loop, symbolizing enlightenment and spiritual powers. She is calm and collected while exhibiting dominion over the fierce lion but her demeanor bestows love and compassion. As stated under the chapter on *Numerology*, the number 8 is also associated with abundance and prosperity, as well as rebirth, regeneration and transformation. At one point in history, the Strength card was entitled "Fortitude," which translates as "strength of mind." Strength is affiliated with the sign of Leo, with the Sun as its ruling planetary body, which epitomize warmth and light.

When Strength appears in a Querent's reading, it communicates personal empowerment that comes through restraint and self-control. Having the courage and fortitude to navigate sticky situations is the key to success. "Your resilience will greatly aid you, and your fearlessness means that you should have no issues speaking your mind."[20]

X. The Hermit.

The Hermit relates to the number "9," representative of the ending of all that has come before in the Earth base ten mathematical system. He stands on a snowy mountain peak looking down upon a valley below. Usually, The Hermit has a long beard and is dressed in a light blue robe or cloak, an indicator of hidden knowledge within, as well as the color gray immersed throughout, a hint at true understanding of the blending of opposites, for gray is the combination of white and black polarities. He holds a lantern, casting away the darkness, with a six-pointed star inside, symbolic of Jewish faith. He holds a staff on his left side. Throughout history, the staff denotes the qualities of authority, guidance, strength, protection, divine power, love and, most importantly, a *tool* for learning. The Hermit communicates a time for self-reflection, and signifies "...the need to look inward and access your own inner wisdom to find your path forward; essentially, a call to delve deep into your own consciousness to seek enlightenment."[21] He is transformation and transmutation surrounding the evolutionary cycle of life. Additionally, The Hermit is affiliated with the Zodiac sign of

---

[20] Quote from "Labyrinthos.com" by Tina Gong dated March 17, 2017.
[21] Reference derived from "https://www.mysticdoorway.com/the-hermit/."

THE BEGINNER'S GUIDE TO METAPHYSICS

Virgo, which displays those characteristics within his nature. This is most understood through both the virtues, dependability and introspection that Virgos bestow in their everyday lives. They are able to amass hidden parts of themselves, as well as Universal understanding through their deep self-awareness, as well as universal analysis and comprehension of exactly "how" the universe works without dependence on outside forces.

When The Hermit presents in a Querent's reading, it symbolizes introspection, for true wisdom is gained only though quiet contemplation, thereby tapping into the energy of the Higher Self. This is where one finds him/her/themselves, accomplished only by the exploration of the shadow side of the self. It is a time to go within, choosing the path of solitude, leaving the 3D world of chaos and distraction behind. One must learn to incorporate the hidden aspects in order to obtain authentication of self. Having faith that everything will unfold as divinely planned is a necessity in order for wisdom to be mastered. This is the key to understanding the messages from Source, which are divulged through one's own intuition, and mark the Ascension into the light.

XI. Wheel of Fortune.

The Wheel of Fortune ("The Wheel") indicates the manifestation of all the hard work of each archetype. As stated in Chapter 3, *Numerology*, the combination of double digits is significant. The Wheel starts the journey anew, incorporating both the number "1," new beginnings, and "0," *The Hero's Journey* toward evolutionary soul progression and enlightenment par excellence. The number one embodies "individuation and self-consciousness,"[22] while the absence of a number, or "0", is the empty set or "eternal nothing."[22] The Wheel encompasses the importance of adaptability and embracing new opportunities, which materialize based upon the efforts made during the journey. The rewards are as great as the discipline, hard work and intentions set forth and made through the continuing, positive aspirations. Truly a reflection of one's resolution toward personal gain on a spiritual level. The Wheel also embraces the

---

[22] Quote from "Mystery Teachings" on Gaia TV by Dr. Theresa Bullard; Season 4, Episode 11, dated December 1, 2020.

dynamic part of our Earthly existence and understanding that life is cyclical. It also demonstrates that positive, life-changing circumstances are about to present but not without the effort of letting go of what no longer serves a purpose. The "out with the old, in with the new" principle of life. This card is also a reminder that everyone has the power within them to design and manifest their own destiny. The Wheel is special because it is also considered a portal, or gateway, toward balance and inner awareness; a marked achievement along *The Hero's Journey* so long as progress is being made on their personal Hero's Journey. The individual ("1") literally walks through the portal, zero ("0") towards transformation. And is "...a return to the unity source."[22] The Wheel of Fortune also has a much deeper meaning in relation to alchemy, mysticism and esoteric wisdom. It is suggested, for those wanting a deeper understanding, to view Dr. Theresa Bullard-Whyke's "Mystery Teachings Season 4, Episode. 11" as found on Gaia TV. Lastly, The Wheel is connected to the planet Jupiter, always referred to as the planet of luck or "Lord of Fortune" but also associated with the elements of air and fire, reflective of the Major Arcana card known as Temperance, which relates to the sun sign of Sagittarius and expansion.

When the Wheel of Fortune presents during a reading, the Querent can expect to be granted a reprieve of sorts in regards to a more positive turn in their life. It is an indication of one's efforts or, in the alternative, a reminder that one cannot sit about on their laurels and expect change to occur without any effort. Sadly, the reaping of one's enterprise toward the divine light is short lived, and one's resolve will be tested. It creates a shift in the atmosphere, usually one that would not have been predicted. If one were to stay within their comfort zone, evolution would cease. Without propulsion (forward movement), one would succumb to lackadaisical style of living. Perhaps, even choosing to discontinue *The Hero's Journey*. It should also be noted that during a reading, The Wheel may also signify a windfall or a loss. Again, fortune comes to those who have a greater good principle of intention. They manifest their destiny through creativity, exertion and by never giving up. One must believe that all desires and intentions *will* come to fruition, for believing results in the seeing the manifestation of one's efforts.

XII. Justice.

Justice is the eleventh (11th) Archetype card presented in the Major Arcana and relates to the ideas and concepts of honesty, truth, justice and balance in order to achieve spiritual success. All the Major Arcana cards that have come before were descending. Justice marks the ascension toward spiritual advancement. This double digit repetition of the number "1" is considered the first master number of the Major Arcana, and contains mystical properties. Justice is shown as a female figure wearing a red robe, which communicates sovereignty, and a gray robe[23] indicative of impartiality, objectivity and neutrality. Justice is also seated between two white pillars akin to that of the High Priestess, which revealed the revelation of polarity and duality that are ever present within this 3D Earthly existence. There is also a purple curtain resting between the pillars, which relates to previous card, the Wheel of Fortune. This "curtain" foretells that Justice is the "Guardian at the Gate" between Earth and the Veil. A golden crown is worn, symbolic of the authority, power, leadership and the dominion over justice. Whenever a gold crown materializes in the Tarot, it is an indication of a high level of achievement and mastery, which also eludes to the crown chakra principle of divine understanding. A double-edged sword is held upright in the right hand, relaying the message that the fairest decision will be made by literally cutting through the issue(s) at hand and without judgment. The scales of justice in the left hand refer to the integrity bestowed by the decision maker but also the requirement by the Querent to accept one's responsibility for their actions, which is directly connected to the laws of karma (i.e., cause and effect). *Cause* has a ripple effect.

Justice is also concurrent with the astrological sign of Libra, portrayed by the scales, the only inanimate symbol depicted in the 12 astrological signs of the Zodiac. Librans do not have a built in equilibrium as do all other signs within the Zodiac. When posed with a question, they must weigh all potential outcomes before making their final choice. To some,

---

[23] Some Justice Tarot cards show green around the neck of Justice. Green is the representation of Masculine energy. When red and green are combine, they create the color gray.

this can appear as indecision; however, rest assured the Libra is pensively calculating the best result.

Justice teaches discernment in *all* things, not just one's actions but also in one's thoughts, words, deeds and emotions. It is balance at its finest and relays the message of how this can best be achieved. When Justice is pulled from the Tarot card deck, the Querent must ask him/her/themselves to view negative circumstance(s) upon its merits and determine the best situation that will restore balance. A task that can appear daunting at times as one's future remains unknown until the decision is made. Fairness is the key to the perfect resolution. The Querent must ask what part he/she/they has played in the disruption of a situation. What is their contribution that has brought about the disturbance or imbalance. How can he/she/they course correct and provide the truth of the matter. What is the best outcome for a spiritual resolution.

XIII. The Hanged Man.

The number "12" is assigned to The Hanged Man of the Major Arcana. The Hanged Man is upside down on a tree that is rooted into Earth and believed to connect the underworld to the heavens. His demeanor is unexpected, as he appears to be in this predicament of his own accord. Some claim that his garments, appearing of no real consequence, are actually a representation of the different aspects of the human experience. The deep, esoteric and symbolic meaning behind this card brings forth the realization that the journey toward ascension can come only through a personal expedition or vision quest, wherein one must experience self-sacrifice in order to obtain self-acceptance. This quest requires shedding the cloak of the material realm in order to reach spiritual knowledge and understanding. Patience is required, along with the surrendering of one's preconceived notions in order to gain new perspectives of universal knowledge. Additionally, this card portrays the highest potential for achievement within a person or a specific situation. Numerologically speaking, the numbers "1, 2" and "3" are presented, with the number "3" being the numbers "1" and "2" added together; therefore The Hanged Man also resonates with all three of the energies of the Magician, High Priestess and Empress. This Tarot card is also allied with the watery planet of Neptune, ruler of inspiration, intuition and the subconscious mind, as well as idealism. The Hanged Man also falls under the purview of Zodiac sign Pisces. When Pisces is found anywhere in one's Natal Chart, it signifies genuine compassion for humanity, and the ability to let go of circumstances beyond one's control in order for the flow of energy to be deemed flexible, as well as versatile.

When the Querent draws The Hanged Man, circumspection and discernment are required in order for wisdom, intuition and spirituality to enter into play. In life, maintaining perspective is one of the most favorable keys to success. One, however, cannot forget that each goal, or situation, must remain rooted in reality and not an unrealistic, dreamlike fantasy or perception.

XIV. Death.

Death is allied with the number "13;" therefore, it is also associated with the numbers "1," "3" and "4." These numbers are integrated within the understanding of the reading via, not only the characteristics of each of the Major Arcana card represented by the Magician, Empress and Emperor respectively, but also their numerological significance as noted in Chapter 3. It should also be noted that "death" implies an ending, which also indicates re-birth in its wake. Letting go of that which no longer serves a purpose is the true meaning to this, often times, misunderstood Tarot card.

The Grim Reaper sits upon a white, or pale, horse wielding a flag emblazoned with The White Rose of York and both dead and dying people from all walks of life below him. In the background are two towers and a rising sun. White, as noted previously, symbolizes purity, while the rose is symbolic of hope. As Earth is based upon the principle of polarity, the positive and negative energy of life are always in flux. Many are fearful of change; however, it is an inevitability. Because change can be difficult, especially for those with fixed signs, outside forces, such as planetary shifts, become necessary in order for movement to occur. Stagnation is not an option.

When a Querent draws the "Death" card it is time for a significant change in order for transformation. What ideology or relationships have become static? Is the job really so important that it is worth the sacrifice of sanity? Now is the time for new opportunities.

XV. Temperance.

The beautiful Tarot card of Temperance is assigned the number "14," which is associated with the numbers "1," "4" and "5." Temperance is associated with the energy of the Magician and his ability to manifest, as well as the ability to wield the power associated with the Emperor. Together, these forces combine the abilities to impart divine wisdom as signified by the Hierophant. In the English language, Temperance refers to moderation or self-restraint, while this may ring true in the Major Arcana, the meaning goes much deeper. The figure presented is androgynous, has the wings of an angel, and wears a flowing white garment with a triangle inside a square at the top center. These two emblems are shapes associated with sacred geometry and the structures of the cosmos. The triangle symbolizes a connection to divine power, while the square relates to stability and grounding. Both these geometric patterns are linked to the two cups of liquid being transported back and forth, all of which symbolize the mastering of alchemy. One foot is firmly planted on the ground, while the other is placed within the water below. There is a pathway in the lower left part of the card where a crown is presented, suggesting the attainment and completion of a goal, perhaps even mastery.

Temperance is associated with the sign of Sagittarius and the planet Jupiter. The Sagittarian connection to Temperance relates to the need and pursuit for both to achieve balance, harmony and moderation in all things, even while enduring opposing forces. In order to reach a state of equilibrium, patience and self-control are necessary.

XVI. The Devil.

The Devil is associated with the number "15." The Devil presents with "harpy feet, ram horns, bat wings, a reversed pentagram on the forehead, a raised right hand and a lowered left hand holding a torch. He squats on a square pedestal. Two naked demons (one male, one female) with tails stand chained to the pedestal."[24] Numerologically, "15" translates to the numbers "1," "5," and "6," incorporating the energies of the Magician, Hierophant and Lovers. When broken down, The Devil, through the energy of the Magician, illustrates the ability to bring together creative ideas by planting seeds and watching them grow. The presentation of these abilities comes through by being the devoted spiritual leader who offers guidance to those within his community, and possibly beyond (i.e., Hierophant). The number 6 is related to Extra Sensory Perception (ESP), and resonates with the planet Venus. Venus is creativity and artistic abilities but also the union between partners. The Devil card shows the opportunity for self-evaluation and cautions against addiction, obsession and entrapment. Upon reaching this archetypal level along *The Hero's Journey*, one must realize he/she/they are responsible for *all* their own actions. If negativity is becoming more prevalent within, and even through outside forces, it is time for reflection.

The Devil in a Querent's reading signifies the need to slow down and assimilate, and to ask the question "How am I personally responsible for any distress and negative emotions surrounding my circumstances?' Where are the imbalances? The Devil card is a reminder to go within regardless the area of life that has become difficult.

XVII. The Tower.

The number "16" is associated with The Tower and the planet Mars. The Tower sits atop a rocky platform with a lightening bolt striking the gold crown that is falling to the ground. This symbolism is indicative of loss of a high level of achievement or mastery due to following a path of materialism. Below the crown, sparking its removal, are flames of danger, destruction and crisis. A person is forced to leave due to the ignition of the flames. The prior card's warning (i.e., The Devil) was dismissed by the Querent, leaving devastation in its wake.

The number 16 resonates with the numbers "1", "6" and "7," implying the Magician, in some way, shape or form, has yielded his power in some

---

[24] Quote taken from "...https://en.wikipedia.org/wiki/The_Devil_(tarot_card)#:~:text=The%20Devil%20(XV)%20is%20the,of%20Marseilles%20by%20Jean%20Dodal."

fashion, perhaps resulting in a bit of a backfire effect. The number six in this triangle relays the message that psychic prowess was utilized recently, and asks the question "Was it used wisely?" or "Was it used to manipulate?" When the number seven emerges, it symbolizes completeness and spiritual awakening. In short, The Tower confirms that, while the Fool has journeyed forth, he/she/they *is* the Magician with great ESP gifts; however, this source of power and psychic abilities must be processed under the rule of "the greater good" or there will be consequences. Knowing the difference is the key toward becoming the master.

A Querent who draws upon The Tower in a reading does not necessarily need to experience the down side of the above portrayal, for the upside to this card is liberation through the letting go, again, of attitudes that are no longer useful, helpful or productive.

Often times for the Querent, this card is drawn to warn one of unforeseen changes. One can choose to embrace this shakeup that by its very essence was done purposefully or one can wallow in self-pity. Again, the Querent's *choice*!

XVIII. The Star.

The Star is another beautifully illustrated Tarot Card from the Rider-Waite deck and concerns the number "17". A naked female figure has her right foot firmly in a pool of water while kneeling on her left knee onto the embankment. She is pouring water from a red jar back into the water. This illustration refers to the water-bearer, or the sun sign of Aquarius, as well as its ruling planet, Uranus. The bright and beautiful sun is shinning amid a blue sky and green grass with seven twinkling, white stars in the backdrop. Her naked body reveals her openness and positive outlook toward renewed hope and faith in the universe. The sun and stars are expressive of the many blessings bestowed and inspired connection to the divine spirit. The Magician's (#1) seeds have bared fruit and manifested spiritual awakening (#7), bringing forth a sense of calm and oneness with the universe. The implication of the number eight (1 + 7 = 8) brings forth serenity and optimism as the cycle of *The Hero's Journey* materializes.

The Querent has reached a place of wonder and amazement along his/her/their journey. All the efforts, trials and tribulations have created a greater understanding of the universe, allowing for a sense of renewal before true completion. This is a sign that the spiritual awareness generated has allowed for emotional, physical and spiritual healing. The Star is also symbolic of wish fulfillment. As one sends intentions out into the vast universe, without caveats or conditions, the universe replies in kind with blessings.

XIX. The Moon.

The Moon is linked with the number "18," with emphasis on its magical qualities as noted by the influence of number one (i.e., the Magician). The design of the number eight increases its relevance and power due to the infinity sign implication. Lastly, the two numbers combined (1+8) total the number nine; the highest number possible under the number ten base system used on Earth. As stated in Chapter 3 on *Numerology*, the number nine is the number of completion and transformation, symbolizing power over a particular obstacle or obstacles, and confirms the finalization of a cycle or an alteration in consciousness.

The Moon is considered a luminary, and is the ruler of the Zodiac sign of Cancer, deeply connected with the element of water. It alternates through every sign of the Zodiac on a monthly basis, approximately every 2.5 days. The Moon reveals the magnitude of its constant influence over human emotions. It is concerned with imagination through intellectual light that is present during each Moon phase or cycle. According to A. E. Waite, the dog and the wolf represent the fears of the natural mind when there is only reflected, not actual, light to be one's guide. Waite's final message is "Peace, be still," wherein one's mind should turn toward inward reflection to help create a calming effect. Without the attempt toward peaceful resolution, the Moon can refer to illusion and deception; however, not in relation to the influences of the outside world, per se, but one's own truth that is difficult to face. Perhaps one has put his/her/their trust in someone undeserving.

In a reading, the Querent should be encouraged to trust their own intuition. Often times people will influence decision making based upon their own selfish needs rather than that of the Querent. These people may

pretend to have the Querent's best interests at heart but truly fall short.
The Moon can symbolize uncertainty and ambiguity, in part due to lack of
information and/or discernment. It is a time for self-reflection like that of
the Hermit, also under the number nine. The Hermit's energy, like that of
the Moon, symbolizes, transformation and transmutation. The completion
of an evolutionary cycle.

XX. The Sun.

The Sun is associated with the number "19." Again exhibiting its
magical qualities through the influence of the number one (i.e., the
Magician). The number 9, as stated prior, is the end of the Earth based
sequencing, which implies completion and finality. The Sun concludes
a long-endured task, possibly graduating from high school or college.
The Sun shines bright, relaying the message of abundance, with a sky
of blue, equaling a happy journey. Sunflowers, symbolic of optimism
and accomplishment, are located below and in the background upon
a concrete, sturdy wall. The face of the Sun shows contentment, and
rightfully so because one's hard work, even tenacity, has paid off. There
is a young, naked child atop a white horse of purity and light. The age
relation is indicative of the inner child of the Querent, ready for fun and
optimistic about his/her/their future.

The Sun is associated by the Zodiac sign of Leo, the lion. Leo shins
bright with a cheerful buoyancy and upbeat attitude. Well, most of the
time! This card stands for those qualities. The Sun always shines bright,
and is a reflection of one's accomplishments. It portends to elicit good
fortune, joy and harmony. In a reading, the Sun reveals the Querent
has hit the Mother Load but not out of shear luck but instead through
concentrated effort. It is a time of celebration; however, it is also a time
of endings, which insinuates new beginnings. The Querent is to enjoy
the ride; however, this card is also a foreshadowing. Once one's former
endeavors have bared fruit, it really means that the next journey is about
to begin for the world in which we live is dynamic.

XXI. Judgment.

The number "20" represents the Tarot card of Judgment and, again, the subject of duality through its number "2" resonance. The true meaning of this card is to stand in "judgment" of oneself, not others. One has walked, learned and grown during *The Hero's Journey*, becoming all the archetypes of human existence. This signifies an understanding of the plight *every* human must endure in order to obtain spiritual growth. When the voyage toward self-discovery is approached in a specific way, personal transformation, spiritual awakening and renewal are the beautiful result. This feeling of accomplishment is joyous and undeniable. Symbolically, there is a new horizon, or rebirth, ahead as one lets go of that which no longer serves a true purpose. It is a time to embrace life and to get ready for new challenges.

The Judgment card depicts the divine messenger that is the Archangel Gabriel, with his light colored hair (or halo) of higher wisdom. He is blowing his trumpet to arouse those lying dormant below, and to inform them the time to understand one's higher state of consciousness has arrived. The white flag with a red cross shown near or under Gabriel's right arm symbolizes a victorious and favorable result. The blue sky of clarity and white mountain peaks covered in snow are symbolic of the insurmountable obstacles that have been overcome through one's determination and gumption in order to reach the new state of consciousness. The blue water is also an indication of clarity and renewal. The naked people below are standing in coffins, rejoicing at their rebirth, or reincarnation, as they venture forth to embrace their future. The nudity demonstrates the vulnerability that occurs when one attempts to shed their old identity.

When Judgment appears before the Querent, it is a time of revitalization, which is evidenced by the absolute end to a specific period of time in one's life. A reminder that the world in which we live is dynamic. While goals, and the outcome measured by such, are important, it is really the journey that matters. As everyone has their own path, which they alone must follow, it is just that; *their path.* No one person needs anyone else's judgment concerning their particular approach to life. This is how humans learn to embrace diversity. One's unique viewpoint of the world, as *he/she/they* see it, leads to creativity, ingenuity and innovation. While there are a set of "rules," they do not interfere with one's *free will*. A key factor on this 3D plane of existence. The life of each human is about the evolutionary soul cycle toward enlightenment and becoming one with Source. The important aspect of this card is to learn to appreciate the blood, sweat and tears that are required toward that end.

XXII. The World.

The World is the final Major Arcana archetype and is associated with the number "21" but is also associated with the "22" letter of the Hebrew alphabet. *The Hero's Journey* is now considered complete, which has been achieved through hard work, determination, self-reflection and evaluation. The actual "change" has occurred with a newness and excitement on the horizon. The numbers "1" and "2," the seeds created by the Magician, and the manifestation of the High Priestess, have come full circle. The World shows a naked woman, which is symbolic of freedom and authenticity, wrapped in a purple cloth who appears to be dancing above the Earth, holding a baton in each hand. Dancing is a form of rejoicing, while the purple cloth relates to stately or elevation of the woman who has finished a marked task. The Magician too held a baton, but she holds two, proof of the absolute fulfillment of her desires. The very large wreath encompassing the woman represents honor, unity and wholeness. An angel sits in the upper left-hand corner, symbolic of a divine, guiding presence that has been present since the beginning. The three remaining corners show animals, the bull (lower left), the eagle (upper right) and the lion (lower right).

The World card in a Querent's reading is extremely significant, not only because it refers to the completion of a cycle but because it also exemplifies integration and transcendence. For every human born, there is an expectation that *something* will be completed during his/her/their lifetime. When this card presents, it infers that a great accomplishment has occurred, and the Querent is permitted to celebrate. It also signifies that, while this is rewarding, the journey will begin again.

In case the readers have yet to realize, this Major Arcana Archetype presentation within this *Beginner's Guide* is based upon the positive or "upright" position of each Tarot card meaning. If interested, one could ponder the negative, upside down positions; however, being on the positive polarity seems to hold a greater understanding of *The Hero's Journey*. When the card is noted in the reverse during a reading, it is meant to allow the Querent the opportunity to turn their intentions toward a more positive outcome.

CHAPTER 8

MICHAEL

"Michael" is an entity made up of approximately 1,050 souls, a collective of warriors and kings that live on the "Causal" plane. The purpose for their teaching is to assist in the understanding of human nature, which is experienced in this Physical, third dimensional plane and exhibited through personality. Accessing, acknowledging and validating one's characteristics creates a foundation for transformation during one's current incarnation on Earth. By sharing *their* divine wisdom, *they* supply insights and clarity regarding the soul's evolutionary process. Their ultimate goal for humanity is for all to become more aware, or conscious, of reality beyond the senses. Through review, analysis and knowledge better decisions with greater insight ensues. An integration of fragments, if you will, "...of a larger entity," or an "entity integrated whole" is how *they* describe themselves (Yarboro, pp. 49, 58). The particular aspect of information *they* depart is truly invaluable. It connects a higher level of dimensional reality to Earth based existence. Their knowledge is epic, and they denote an integral aspect on the "how to approach" to life by allowing one to visualize and grasp the positive and negative aspects of their personality. This, along with their wide array of instruction, aids in one's individual soul quest.

Earth is a Third Dimensional plane of reality. The Causal plane (5th Dimension) sits "above" the Fourth Dimensional Astral Plane, which is considered the human "dream state." The Fifth Dimensional plane "is an upward state of spiritual evolution" (Yarbro, p. 146), and what is considered the most vital course of action for Earthlings. The Ascension of the human spiritual path can no longer be denied. The dense energy of a the Third Dimension prevents spiritual growth. It has become detrimental. Like energy, which is dynamic, so is our spiritual expansion. The ebb and flow, or positive and negative polarities of being human, is the point of an Earth based soul's journey. The truth of life comes in similar fashion – through the gradual movement of energy and progression. While one walks through the adventure known as "life," never forget that discernment is the key. What rings true for one, may not be true for another; however, there are important facets of universal laws that require adherence.[25]

According to Michael, all souls are fragments of Source. Michael's definition of "Source" is the easiest to understand. An analogy is provided by Michael on page 57 of *Messages From Micheal* (25th Anniversary Edition) by author, Chelsea Quinn Yarboro. The imagery begins with the filing of ten, airtight and watertight test tubes (i.e., considered the "fragments"), followed by a toss into the Atlantic Ocean. While each test tube is a representation of an individual "fragment of Source," they co-exist in an encapsulated state while under water but "...they are remote for the source and trapped in an effective prison...", in the exact "...same way the soul is trapped in the body" (Yarboro, p. 57). This brings us around to the true limitations of our earthbound nature, which is *only* for the sole purpose of the evolution of consciousness; the soul's true journey.

Michael teachings have a strong connection to the base number seven. There are seven "archetypes" assigned to the casting off of fragments from the Tao. An "archetype" according to Dictionary.com is defined as "the original pattern or model from which all things of the *same* kind are copied or on which they are based." Each grouping of fragments carry seven different personifications of human prototypes. This is the *only* constant throughout the Earth based souls travel. They are as follows: (1) Warrior; (2) Server; (3) Artisan; (4) Scholar; (5) Sage; (6) Priest; and (7) King. While some of these archetypes appear archaic, the definitions given later will explain, in greater detail, the role of each personality, or "camouflage for the body" (Yarboro, p. 61). The role is determined by the number at which the fragment was cast from the Tao. Each fragment also has a secondary characteristic added at the time of casting. For instance, Sage frequency is first cast from the Tao with the secondary aspect of the personality as any one of the other seven, such as a Sage/Warrior, King/Scholar, Server/Artisan, which gives a specific cadence to each archetype. Another layer to

---

[25] These "rules" or "principles" will be discussed in the next book, "The Advanced Guide to Metaphysics."

one's personality or an additional emphasis to the fragment. Each fragment then chooses its "Overleaves," or aspects of personality.

Dr. Linda Backman, an advanced Earth based soul, also has an affinity for the number seven. On "Open Minds" with Regina Meredith, Season 27, Episode 7, on Gaia TV, Dr. Backman discusses the "Seven Soul Archetypes," which have a direct correlation to the Michael teachings. While her seven archetypes vary from those described by Micheal, they do overlap. Margarete Ward is another spiritual author who discusses the concept of young and old souls; however, her idea is a bit more limiting. She writes that "[i]f this earth is the first planet a spirit has made his debut on, he is indeed a young soul" (p. 71). Adding that "[a]s a rule, a soul living its first life on earth and never having lived on another planet,[26] has a harder struggle to exist than an older soul who has lived a number of previous lives either on earth, or on another planet" (p. 71). The older soul exhibits a more broadened view of humanity, as well as a greater tolerance for the many mistakes humans make along their adventure towards enlightenment. In Michael terms, the soul begins the journey on Earth by starting at the level of the Infant, which starts at first breath. The Infant Soul travels through at least seven different levels before reaching the next – the Baby Soul. The pathway follows a minimum of seven different lifetimes, each fraught with their own specific lessons, bringing about joy and pain, often times in equal measure. From the Baby Soul, one incarnates into the Young Soul. From here, one moves toward the Mature Soul experience. Upon completion of Mature Soul lives, which are considered among the most difficult lessons to learn, one moves toward being an Old Soul, the last of the physical incarnations on the Physical Earth plane. The sixth and seventh levels become Transcendental. One then exits in the ethereal realm(s) of consciousness, where they are only of "service to others;" its opposite considered "service to self."

Before continuing with the concept of "Overleaves," clarification of one's archetypal role and soul levels should be addressed. In case one hasn't noticed, there are a few central theme's that run throughout this enchanting metaphysical expedition. Micheal has a way of bringing polarity to the forefront of their teachings, as well as numerology. "There are seven

---

[26] Again, galactic awareness is obviously related to a more highly evolved, other dimensional level of existence.

88

levels of evolution of the soul, five of which manifest in the Physical plane" (Yarboro, p. 61). As stated prior, the archetypes do not change from lifetime to lifetime. They represent the consistency, or grounding effect, of being human. Michael refers to this as "The Nature of the Soul." During the first publication of this extremely relevant text, the psychiatrists of the time would have termed such "levels of awareness" as a representation of the "subconscious," or "essence." Michael, however, imparts that all souls, or fragments, are "...a part of the universal creative force," which they call the Tao (Yarboro, p. 57). When "...fragmentation occurs and the physical cycle begins," each fragment has a type of detachment from Source. Michael adds that "...physicality is as much a part of evolution as what you call 'spirituality,' and neither state is more 'advanced' or 'laudable' than the other" (p. 57). The Ascension of consciousness in cosmic circles is "essential to evolution" (p. 57). One must remember; "[t]he soul in its true spiritual state has no limitations or handicaps; therefore, the soul is capable of living in all dimensions simultaneously" (p. 57). Restrictions occur when one doesn't embrace the purpose of being human: To experience polarity, duality and the balance of the two over many lifetimes. This is a very problematic concept for humans to grasp, largely due to the programming, or "imprinting," that infiltrates perception from the moment of birth. In sociological terms, "imprinting" refers to the social mores of the day. What your grandparents taught your parents, whom, in turn, passed down to you. It is also ancestral, deeply linked to your DNA heritage. One must never forget that humans are complex creatures. The more one comprehends the multi-faceted and multi-dimensional aspects of self, along with the complexity of existence, the more difficult it can become to be discerning. One's soul is separate from personality, "...which is for the most part a survival mechanism for the body" (Yarboro, p. 58). This "survival mechanism" is intact for a specific reason. It is the human "fight or flight" DNA and "ego" related response. Although there is less need for this in today's world, at one point it was an absolute necessity. This reaction causes conflict for the progression of the soul. "This is a bittersweet sweet symphony, this life"[27] (The Verve). "Only the soul can ask the question 'Why am I here?' The personality does not require such information"

---

[27] Musicians have a way of taking "reality" into the spiritual realm with shear and utter beauty and delight!

(Yarboro, p. 58). The Soul Cycles are extensive in description. For the purposes of this *Beginner's Guide*, each will be highlighted in short detail in *Chart No. 8.1* below.

Chart No. 8.1

SOUL CYCLES	DESCRIPTION
Infant or *Firstborn*	*Motto*: "Let's Not Do It." ˗ World Perception = "Me" & "Not Me" (Yarboro, pp. 61-62) ★Limited Range of Perception and Activities ★Find Complexity Frightening ★Manifest Fear Through Exaggeration ★Unaware of Right/Wrong but Can Be Taught ★Generally Do Not Seek Higher Education ★ Bewildered & Hostile in Strange Situations ★Appear Mentally Lacking & Mentally Deficient ★Adopt Religious Beliefs of Parents ★Lack Culinary Skills, Cooking is Only for Survival ★Fearful ★Unadventurous or Curious due to Fear Base Understanding
Baby	*Motto*: "Do It Right or Not at All." ★ World Perception = "Me" & "Many Other Me's" (Yarboro, pp. 62-63) ★More Complex ★ Forms Strong Beliefs in Early Childhood, Borrowed from Outside Sources that Become Unshakable ★Normally Agreeable Unless Belief System is Challenged ★Seek to be Big Fish in Small Pond ★Preservation of Status Quo is of Utmost Importance ★ Religious Fundamentalist, Believe in Forces of Evil ★Seen as Prudish ★Not Connoisseurs but Understand Nutrition ★Ashamed of Sexuality ★Manifest Psychological Distress through Physical Symptoms ★Prone to Utilization of Courts when Sense of Justice has been Outrageously Insulted ★Terrified of Being Out of Body ★ Guileless

Chart No. 8.1 - Continued

SOUL CYCLES	DESCRIPTION
	Motto: "Do It My Way." ˉ World Perception = "Me as Me" & "You as You" Perception here is really about differences. While I am "me" and "you are you," "you" are most definitively *different from me*! (Yarboro, pp. 63-64) These life experiences are considered an adventurous time as the soul begins to venture into new territory. It is akin to the teenage years, where exploration is the norm and emotions are at the forefront. * * *
Young	★Movers & Shakers of the World ★Architects of Civilization ★ Experience the Need to Change & Persuade You into Being More Like Them ★Almost Always Seeks Higher Education ★Tireless Worker for a Cause ★Achievement of the Utmost Importance ★Religious Pursuits Tend Toward Extreme Orthodoxy[28] ★If Perception of Sexual Prowess is Low, they Spend Time Attempting to Convince Others that Sex is Evil ★If Invested in Sexual Freedom, they Perceive Love is Eros, which can Create High Expectations, making for Agonizing Sexual Conflicts "– early training versus internal urge" (Yarboro, p. 63) ★Early-Cycles have a Tendency to Adhere to the Food Traditions Learned in Childhood; Late-Cycles Experiment, "...and food fetishes often develop" (Yarboro, p. 64) ★Owners of "Status" Pets ★Engage in the Rodeo ★Attracted to the Physical Body ★Incarnate at a Faster Pace, Finding that Being Out of the Body to be Unpleasant ★Always in a State of Unrest

---

[28] Orthodoxy refers to the practice of adherence to an established indoctrination.

	Motto: "Do It Any Place But Here." ★ World Perception = "Perceives Others as They Perceive Themselves" (Yarboro, pp. 64-66) As stated previously, this particular aspect of the evolutionary cycles of being human are most difficult, "...demanding much introspection and often seeming to give little peace in return" (Yarboro, p. 64). The Young Soul Cycle, with its many "choices," has a tendency to cause karmic debts, especially when many Young souls have yet to comprehend the true meaning of cause and effect. Mature Souls are also able to "...perceive the unhappy ones," causing the "...desire to shield themselves from the unpleasant vibrations...", for which there is no recourse, regardless of efforts made on their behalf (Yarboro, p. 64). The "It is what it is" principle.
Mature	* * * ★ Perceives Beauty with Clarity ★ Sees "Truth" at End of Cycle, which Cannot be Denied ★ Seek and Question Motivations of All ★ Expansion of Consciousness through Opening of Brain Wave Patterns ★ Psychic Abilities Present with Increased Frequency and Intensity ★ Serious Spiritual Work Begins ★ While Increased Perception Emerges, Understanding Doesn't Necessarily Follow[29] ★ Acute Perception of Dimensional Realms ★ Heightened Dream State with Visual Acuity ★ Always Seeking, Often Times without Rhyme nor Reason ★ Beset with Many Issues, All Intrinsic ★ Require Sanctuary and Respite ★ Seeks Higher Education in All Formats ★ Makes Large Contribution to Areas of Knowledge, Both Philosophical and Scientific ★ "Seeks Quiet Faiths" ★ If Inner Conflicts are Resolved, can be Ardent Lover with Deep and Lasting Potential ★ "Enjoy Precision Cooking and Gourmet Dining"

---

[29] Many at this evolutionary cycle may consider themselves an "Empath;" however, this is not necessarily true as this phase is linked to a reflection of the higher sensitivity to universal truths.

THE BEGINNER'S GUIDE TO METAPHYSICS

	Motto: "You Do What You Want and I'll Do What I Want." ★ World Perception = "Perceives Others as a Part of Something Greater that Includes Self." (Yarboro, pp. 65-66)
Old	★ Spiritual Quest is *All* that Matters ★ Newer, More Profound Creativity in All Things ★ Seeks Route of Least Resistance ★ Enjoy Hard Manual Labor! ★ Not as Concerned with Higher Education, Unless Required Under Chosen Profession ★ Many are Gardeners ★ Realize Futility & Temporary Nature of Material Achievements ★ All Extremely Competent, with Endless Capabilities and Potential ★ Flip Side, No Motivation ★ Religion is "Expansive" and Includes Unorthodox Rituals ★ Casual About Sex but "Intensely Sensual" ★ Creative Cooks, Love Spices & Herbs ★ Inspire Confidence in Animals, for which Animals Respond in Kind ★ Find Comfort in Relationships with Animals, even the Wild ★ All Come to Philosophy and the Arts ★ Searching for Home ~ Connections to All Fragments within Their Specific Entity Cast from the Tao ★Wisdom is Reflected Through Eyes

Chart No. 8.1 – Continued

SOUL CYCLES	DESCRIPTION
Transcendental & Infinite	*Motto*: Being Nonphysical, Except in Times of Manifestations, these High Souls Need No Motto! (Yarboro, pp. 68-69) *Transcendental* ★Experiences Others as Itself ★Exalted Souls ★Telepathic Rapport and Psychic Union ★Precede Descent of Realized Masters by Less Than 100 Years ★Can Walk-In and Enter Physical Body of Old Soul at Any Time During the Life Cycle ★Provoke Need of Spiritual, Philosophical or Cultural Revolution ★Perceives the Synthesis and Teaches Perception ★Does Not Pursue Physical Union *Infinite* ★Perceives the Tao ★Has Direct Access to *All* Knowledge, Having No Need for Education of Any Type ★Religion is Logos ★Does Not Pursue Physical Union ★Does Not Come to Lead but Dispenses Knowledge and Wisdom; It is Up to the Human to Listen and Take Action

In 1981, Michael revealed one of the most relevant pieces of information received at this stage of human subsistence: "No more entities have been cast onto this planet, into either your human specifics or cetaceans, although, of course, such casting continues on other planets and into other species" (Yarboro, p. 69). Additional pertinent intel is the notation that "[t]here is an end point, of course, to all worlds, when the star exhausts itself."[30] The direction toward fifth dimensional reality is, again, inevitable. The only consistency in life is its inconsistency. Humanity, Earth and all her creatures are in a constant state of expansion.

The next step on the Michael journey involves "The Levels Within The Soul Cycles," which relates to the seven Cycles of soul ages, which Michael relays as "...a matter of perception and function" (Yarboro, p. 73). The first level (Infant Soul[31]), at each stage, only allows for basic growth of

---

[30] Further data concerning our galaxy, and all its inhabitants, will be dispensed in another non-fiction book to be written in the near future. Stay tuned for *The Beginner's Guide To The Galaxy*!

[31] Reference of Soul level is an indicator of the resonance between the two (i.e., the first level of human existence is relative to that of an Infant Soul, second level is Baby Soul, etc.)

the individual, who acts and responds "...without any real perspective on the nature of its actions" (p. 73). Think of it this way. Education begins at a basic level as well. In the United States, for instance, formal instruction begins in Kindergarten, which is really more about the socialization of our species. There is interaction and formal learning, like numbers and our alphabet; however, it is simplistic. This is done purposely, as a form of integration into the social mores of the times. The second level (Baby Soul) of the Cycle is a learning curve of responses with the ability to compare one thing to another, albeit in small increments. Level three (Young Soul) is meant to increase one's discernment with the ability to evaluate situations and circumstances "...with more awareness of the ramifications of [one's] actions" (Yarboro, p. 74). The fourth level (Mature Soul) allows for the gathering of knowledge "and establishes a foundation on which to build" (p. 74). "At the fifth level (Old Soul), integration begins and all that has gone before is understood within the context of the nature of the Cycles" (p. 74). Consciousness integrates at the sixth level (a/k/a, Mature Soul Cycle), and is considered the most difficult phase throughout each soul incarnation. The Mature Soul feels this particular aspect of one's journey exponentially. The most difficult karmic cleansing must be completed during this level in order for the inculcation of the whole pattern of the Cycle to be integrated before moving forward, which is presented at the seventh level.

Understand that "[s]oul level is the function of the Physical plane," and also the "...soul is not of the Physical plane" (Yarboro, p. 75). This infers this is an Earth principle, not a galactic one! Michael also speaks about "gender." Michael states: "How could [the Physical plane] possibly have gender and what good would it be? There is no gender to an entity, and the fragments[32] of an entity have no gender. Male and female are factors of the Physical plane." (p. 75). Additionally, "intellect is not a factor in any of the Cycles" and, "generally," each level requires a minimum of two hundred, non-continuous lives on the Physical plane (p. 75). Fortunately, no one is "judged" for any path chosen. "Every fragment is accountable to itself for its own essence..." (Yarboro, p. 71).

The next area to be covered are "The Roles in Essence." On the Physical plane, the Role (i.e., behavioral patterns) fall under one of three parings, equaling the number six, with the last remaining one considered as neutral (neither positive or negative). They consist of the following combinations, each with their own specific polarity: 1) Sage/Artisan, representing

---

[32] "Fragments" are also referred to as "Soul Shards."

Expression; 2) Priest/Slave, associated with *Inspiration*; 3) King/Warrior, affiliated with *Action*; and 4) The "neutral" Role of the Scholar, whose primary purpose is *Assimilation*. "From the time an entity is cast from the Tao to the time it reunites, the essence or Role of the individual soul does not change" (Yarboro, p. 84). In other words, once a Sage always a Sage until reuniting with Source. None of these designations imply a particular social, political, economic, "or other 'worldly' significance" (p. 84). "Just as the soul level of the soul manifests inwardly, as perception, so the major Role in essence manifests outwardly in attitudes and behavior"[33] (p. 84). Briefly, each of their characteristics is noted below in *Chart No. 8.2.*

Chart No. 8.2   (Yarboro, pp. 84-85)

ROLE	DESCRIPTION
King	✱ King is the Warrior Exalted ✱ Expression through Leadership ✱ Influence Motivation ✱ Take Charge through Knowledge and Inherent Power ✱ Seeks to Guide & Rule ✱ Sees World as his/her/their Realm
Warrior	✱ Expression through Leadership ✱ Influence Motivation ✱ Take Charge through Instinctive Drive ✱ Seeks to Command & Explore ✱ Sees World as Unconquered Territory
Priest	✱ Priest is the Server Exalted ✱ Service to Mankind ✱ Exude Humanitarian Ideals ✱ Sense of God Consciousness ✱ Other Worldliness ✱ Seeks Higher Ideals ✱ Sees World as their "Congregation"
Server	✱ Service to Mankind ✱ Exude Humanitarian Ideals ✱ Seeks Person or Institution to be of Service ✱ Sees World as "Honored Guests" ✱ Greatest Number of Souls on Earth
Sage	✱ Sage is the Artisan Exalted ✱ Manifests through Self-Expression ✱ Innate Wisdom and Sagacity[34] ✱ Searches Unique Things ✱ World is Audience ✱ Accumulates Knowledge "...like a sea sponge" ✱ Extemporaneous Orator
Artisan	✱ Represent Freshness and Originality ✱ Always Creating the Uniqueness of the "Thing" ✱ World is Model
Scholar	✱ Intermediate Role ✱ Observer Æ Participant ✱ Life is Vicarious ✱ Exude Subdued Enthusiasm ✱ Always Seeking New Knowledge ✱ Old Scholar is detached, Aloof and Often Arrogantly Intellectual

---

[33] Original spelling was in English as "behaviour" but changed to American English spelling "behavior."

[34] Someone with acuteness of mental discernment and soundness of judgment.

According to Micheal, one's "Role" is chosen, not assigned, and flows in an "orderly progression" (Yarboro, p. 85). Each soul shard chooses their Earth archetype once cast from the Tao. Additionally, one's Role in Essence is *not* necessarily connected to one's actual life Role, one's essence *is* the soul, "...that part of you which is immortal and eternal," and one's Role only concerns intervals spent on the Physical plane (Yarboro, p. 86).

The last area of exploration in the Michael teachings relates to one's "Overleaves," which *they* refer to as the "Nature of the Soul"; a reflection of one's true self, not false personality or ego. "In other words, the overleaves are the body, the essence is the bones, and false personality is the clothing. Only the overleaves are truly part of you" (Yarboro, p. 92). They represent true personality, which allows one "...to experience all that is necessary...to accomplish a full evolution through the Physical plane" (p. 92). Overleaves vary from lifetime to lifetime in order for one "...to experience the entire range of human life, so that real understanding may occur" (p. 92). Overleaves consist of one's life Goal, accomplished through one's operational Mode, or modus operandi. One's Mode defines how one is able to reach their Goal. The Attitude one chooses is reflective of the stance one takes while attempting their Goal, as well as how one tackles their approach to the matters of being human. Centering relates to how one responds to the outside world. "It indicates from what part of yourself you will act" (Yarboro, p. 96). Lastly, the Chief Feature is what Michael considers that part of your personality which is *flawed*. The "go to" of negative responses. All the Overleaves – one's true personality – work within the framework of polarity.

The *Charts* listed on the next few pages represent the definition of each of the Overleaves noted above with their key word identifier and the positive and negative aspects for which each soul may vacillate throughout each of their Earth lifetimes. While staying within the positive pole may be more appealing, and frankly gain better reactions from the outside world, it is not always that easy. Remember, polarity is at the base of one's existence on the Physical plane.

Chart No. 8.3 (Yarboro, p. 99)

REFLECTION	GOALS	DESCRIPTION	
Expression	Acceptance	+ Polarity is **Agape.**	− Polarity is **Ingratiation.**
	Rejection	+ Polarity is **Discernment.**	− Polarity is **Prejudice.**
Inspiration	Growth	+ Polarity is **Comprehension.**	− Polarity is **Confusion.**
	Retardation	+ Polarity is **Atavism.**	− Polarity is **Withdrawal.**
Action	Dominance	+ Polarity is **Leadership.**	− Polarity is **Dictatorship.**
	Submission	+ Polarity is **Devotion.**	− Polarity is **Subservience.**
Assimilation	Stagnation	+ Polarity is **Suspension.**	− Polarity is **Inertia.**

Chart No. 8.4 (Yarboro, p. 100)

REFLECTION	MODES	DESCRIPTION	
Expression	Power	+ Polarity is **Authority.**	− Polarity is **Oppression.**
	Caution	+ Polarity is **Deliberation.**	− Polarity is **Phobia.**
Inspiration	Passion	+ Polarity is **Self-Actualization.**	− Polarity is **Identification.**
	Repression	+ Polarity is **Restraint.**	− Polarity is **Inhibition.**
Action	Aggression	+ Polarity is **Dynamism.**	− Polarity is **Belligerence.**
	Perseverance	+ Polarity is **Persistence.**	− Polarity is **Immutability.**
Assimilation	Observation	+ Polarity is **Clarity.**	− Polarity is **Surveillance.**

Chart No. 8.5 (Yarboro, p. 101)

REFLECTION	ATTITUDES	DESCRIPTION
Expression	Idealist	+ Polarity is **Coalescence.** – Polarity is **Abstraction.**
	Skeptic	+ Polarity is **Investigation.** – Polarity is **Suspicion.**
Inspiration	Spiritual	+ Polarity is **Verification.** – Polarity is **Faith.**
	Stoic	+ Polarity is **Tranquility.** – Polarity is **Resignation.**
Action	Realist	+ Polarity is **Perception.** – Polarity is **Supposition.**
	Cynic	+ Polarity is **Contradiction.** – Polarity is **Denigration.**
Assimilation	Pragmatist	+ Polarity is **Practicality.** – Polarity is **Dogma.**

Chart No. 8.6 (Yarboro, p. 102)

REFLECTION	CENTERS	DESCRIPTION
Expression	Higher Intellectual	+ Polarity is **Truth.** – Polarity is **Telepathy.**
	Intellectual	+ Polarity is **Insight.** , – Polarity is **Reasoning.**
Inspiration	Higher Emotional	+ Polarity is **Love.** – Polarity is **Intuition.**
	Emotion	+ Polarity is **Perception.** – Polarity is **Sentimentality.**
Action	Moving	+ Polarity is **Productive.** – Polarity is **Frenetic.**
	Sexual	+ Polarity is **Integration.** – Polarity is **Desire.**
Assimilation	Instinctive	+ Polarity is **Aware.** – Polarity is **Mechanical.**

Chart No. 8.7 (Yarboro, p. 103)

REFLECTION	CHIEF FEATURE	DESCRIPTION	
Expression	Greed	+ Polarity is **Egotism**.	– Polarity is **Voracity**.
	Self-Destruction	+ Polarity is **Sacrifice**.	– Polarity is **Immolation**.
Inspiration	Arrogance	+ Polarity is **Pride**.	– Polarity is **Vanity**.
	Self-Deprecation	+ Polarity is **Humility**.	– Polarity is **Abasement**.
Action	Impatience	+ Polarity is **Audacity**.	– Polarity is **Intolerance**.
	Martyrdom	+ Polarity is **Selflessness**.	– Polarity is **Mortification**.
Assimilation	**Stubbornness**	+ Polarity is **Determination**.	– Polarity is **Obstinacy**.

This chapter is a dedicated learning tool for the understanding of the natural diversity of humans. We are all on the natural path to Ascension (5D); however, those who are unable to rise to the occasion will reincarnate onto another planet where the Third Dimensional realm still exists. It is a *choice*. We have the *free will* to choose how to reach this necessary goal in order to reach a higher level of spiritual existence. It is also important to remember that a "...soul cannot exceed the limits of its growth" (Yarboro, p. 86). Because linear time is how progression is perceived in this human existence, skipping over how one interprets growth can not exist in this realm. One cannot go from A to Z instantaneously, only from A to B, B to C, C to D, etc. What path will you choose?

CHAPTER 9

INTUITION

Everyone is born with a sixth sense. Children do not have the filters adults have developed over time due to societal input. They are like sponges, soaking up all types of mystical and magical information, and without judgment. If their parents are not open to the paranormal, esoteric principles, mysticism, divination and metaphysics, they may not have the opportunity to promote their gifts to their full potential. In turn, this may send them down a path that does not allow his/her/their Authentic Self to materialize; the greatest disservice to humanity. Some individuals who are born with an innate ability to see beyond what is representative of our Third Dimensional universe are able to tap into gifts at an early age. Again, everyone is intuitive. The development of one's gifts usually starts with a gut reaction to simple "yes" or "no" questions. That feeling one gets when something is known without explanation and beyond reasoning. Sadly, this aspect is often dismissed. Intuition is reality personified. It is just a matter of figuring out the way in which one's Higher Self, and Guides, are attempting communication. The best definition of one's Higher Self is described as the part of you that lives in the Spiritual Realm. While one's soul is always connected to the physical body, it is also simultaneously attached to that part that lives in ethereal, crystalline or spiritual form. One's Higher Self is with the physical part of everyone 24/7. It is that part of one's being that is heart connected and heart centered to the physical body. It is the most loving aspect of one's being. It is that voice in one's head, or gut reaction, that provides truth.

Intuition and psychic abilities are considered *one* and the *same*. Over the course of the past few decades, the term "intuitive" has been more widely accepted than the term "psychic." Aside from the gut reaction principle, where intuition literally comes to the forefront, intuition presents in several forms known as the *"Clairs."* While there are many books on how to hone in on psychic or intuitive abilities, the clairs represent "clarity" through specific means. The clair prefix is derived from the French word meaning "clear." Most books or online references discuss the idea of four clairs; however, there are actually eight: 1) Clairvoyance; 2) Clairaudience; 3) Clairgustance; 4) Clairolfactory; 5) Claircognizance; 6) Clairsentience; 7) Clairempathy; and, 8) Clairtangency. Developing one's clair senses often requires training, whether through a teacher or in the form of personal meditative practices. There are also several books that discuss ways in which one can sharpen specific *"clair"* abilities.

Before continuing with the Clairs, it is also important to clarify the difference between a *"medium"* and a psychic or intuitive. Mediums have the ability to speak with other beings in different realms of existence, including loved one's whom have passed away. A true *medium* will also be capable of utilizing the Akashic Records to gain access to past, present and future events relating to one's loved ones. A more detailed explanation of the Akashic Records is provided in Chapter 10. All mediums are psychic; however, not all psychics are mediums. Mediums can either channel information directly or may go into a trance-like state. In the mid-20th Century, Edgar Cayce, known as "The Sleeping Prophet," would go into a trance and channel medical advise to those in need. He also "...gave approximately twenty-five thousand 'life readings'[,] which chronicled previous incarnations (Montgomery, p. 85). Upon awakening, he would have no recollection of what had transpired. In 1931, Cayce, along with his wife Gertrude, created the Association for Research and Enlightenment, which is still active today. If this particular topic rings a bell, it is highly recommended an investigation into Cayce's works ensue, and his association with the Akashic Records be forthcoming. The trance-like state brings forth a being (or beings) from different ethereal locations within the Milky Way Galaxy. Perhaps, even beyond!

Channeling is another modality for Intuitives. It involves the receiving of information that one "...'translates' according to your interpretation, intelligence, level of understanding and consciousness."[35] Remaining in a

---

[35] Akashic Records Course Level 1 Manual created by Maria Elena Mexia in class offered December 6-8, 2024.

neutral state, without judgment, analyses or interpreting according to one's own beliefs is vital. Indeed this is an essential requirement. Channeling can also occur by way of communicating with inter-dimensional beings, one's Higher Self and Spirit Guides or through a direct representation of the Querent's Higher Self. They way in which detailed information presents itself is dependent upon the interpreter. Again, this can be done automatically through writing or speaking with an intuitive, via a medium who connects in the same way or via trance.

The Clairs.

Clairvoyance is probably the most familiar of the clairs and indicates "clear seeing." This was Cayce's specific gift of insight. This form of intuitive "sight" can manifest through pictures shown through the minds eye, like a movie, through a series of pictures that may flash in slow motion or through seeing visual information. Depending upon the person, their eyes may be open or closed and project REM sleep patterns. *Clairaudience* is "clear hearing," such as a word or phrase that usually comes in the form of a whisper. According to author, wisdom teacher and Runes Master, Kaedrich Olsen,[36] a low vibrational being will tend to repeat the same thing over and over, while a higher vibrational being will use very few words to convey the message. These messages come from one's Higher Self, Higher Spirit Guides, Masters, Light Beings and loved ones whom have entered our 3D realm from a different dimensional existence. Olsen also states that those with this gift may hear a buzzing sound before the words become clear. *Clairgustance* refers to a sense of taste (clear "tasting"), while *Clairolfactory* a sense of smell. These types of clair senses are usually more prevalent in those who specialize in the healing arts. Those with Clairgustance can literally "smell" disease. Smells or tastes that remind us of a loved one is the representation that they are nearby and are an indicator that loved ones are present. *Claircognizance* is a bit more complicated as it invokes "clear knowing," defying all that is "seen" in 3D. This is not necessarily a "gut" feeling, although that can also present, but simply

---

[36] Reference from lecture series *Open Minds* with Regina Meredith (2022), Season 21, Episode 2.

hearing a word, phrase or statement that rings "true," oftentimes without explanation. Additionally, inspiration or creative thoughts come through without rhyme nor reason. Claircognizance involves sudden insights and strong intuition. As such, in ancient times, people with this particular intuitive gift often played crucial roles as oracles, seers, prophets and/or healers within their communities. When asked a specific question, or requesting information on a specific topic, a Claircognizant person will simply know whether or not what is being asked is possible, improbable, true or false. Those who are *Clairsentient* ("clear feeling") feel or sense other people (or beings) energy, while psychics with *Clairemphathy* are equipped with a heightened emotional frequency. Another term utilized for those who exhibit Clairemphathy is an *"Empath."* Often times the empath will be unable to differentiate between their own emotions and those of others without practice and tools to help dissipate the energy. *Clairtangency*, also known as psychometry, is the ability to receive information by touch. Those exhibiting this particular ability can get a sudden insight about the history of an object, person, animal or place when they physically touch it. Lastly, an intuitive will generally bestow more than one clair ability while engaging in a reading. Usually one clair is prominent with one or two additional clairs incorporated, which helps to generate a *clearer* picture. Some psychics are even able to tap into *all* the clairs.

It is said that one must trust the goosebumps rush (Olsen, 2022). This is a distinct universal notification that validates one bestowing the information is on the right path. For some, simply thinking about a question (or questions) and asking for assistance brings about a mysterious response from the Universe that clears the path for circumstance and opportunity. Listed below are a few tools that can assist with the journey towards finding and developing one's clairs senses.

The Pendulum.

The initial use of a pendulum was for the purpose of regulating a clocks movement and has a mathematical formula and relates to the earth's gravity. The formula for the period T of a pendulum is $T = 2\pi$ Square root of $\sqrt{L/g}$, where L is the length of the pendulum and "g" is the acceleration due to gravity. "A simple pendulum consists of a bob suspended at the end of a thread that is so light as to be considered massless" (Britannic, 2014). There are many types and sizes of pendulums with which to choose. The best is one that is shorter and lighter in weight. According to expert, Maria Elena Mexia, "[t]he pendulum is the best tool for leaving the mind blank and neutral and focusing on specific questions, giving space to the answer that is the best solution for you or that contains the answer you are seeking from a truth that comes from...a source of light." [35] The benefit of this simple divination tool is its accurate responses to "yes," "no" or "maybe" questions, which can be a fantastic learning device. If just becoming aware of your "clairs," and a tool would help in understanding the truth of a subject, or for clarification of what your Higher Self and other beings are attempting to convey, this is an easy way to find out whether you are on the right track.

How To Use.

It is wise to set intentions with every new pendulum purchased, and then set aside time to program it prior to usage. The first item on the agenda is to hold the pendulum between the thumb and index finger of the dominant hand, while suspended over the palm of the other. This way of holding is symbolic of divine energy between you, Earth, and the heavens. Ask the pendulum to show you the "yes" response, followed by the "no," and finishing with the direction of the "unknown" response. It is best to first ask questions that you already know are "yes" or "no." It will show you that the pendulum does indeed work. Then to program your pendulum recite the following request as provided by Akashic Records Instructor, Maria Elena Mexia:

> Through my Higher Self, I place upon this pendulum the intention that it only transmit information to me from my Higher Self, unless I specifically give permission for it to be otherwise. May the information that flows be for my highest good and the highest good of all beings. Thank you![35]

Once you have received confirmation, begin your journey toward illumination.

The best way to truly know if this works is to utilize it by testing the information on things that do not have an emotional investment. Often times, one's ego can and does enter the picture. In turn, the heart may also react, causing doubt. Humans are complex beings. There is so much more to a person than their superficial "ego" (a/k/a: "The Protector"). With practice, this small, simple and inexpensive tool will blow your mind. It can, and will, provide specificity and lucidity during one's intuitive journey.

Meditation.

As stated throughout this book, meditation is key to understand the multi-dimensional Universe because it allows time to reset one's energetic field. Dr. Dispenza discusses the "sweet spot of the generous present moment," which refers to living within one's own electromagnetic field (Dispenza, pp. 55-56). Again, the central purpose of meditation. It allows the diversion of one's energy from "...the past and predictable future..." (Dispenza, p. 55). By taking energy away from the outer (outside) world concerns, where time and space exist, and entering the electromagnetic field of the inner world, the constraints of 3D reality are eliminated. As such, meditative techniques allow for the extension of vast benefits of the spiritual and intuitive aspects while investigating and learning how to hone in on your specific clair gifts. There are a few books that can assist with types of meditation geared toward a specific clair that may be useful. Emily Stroia's book *Psychic Development for Beginners: A Practical Guide to Developing Your Intuition & Psychic Gifts* provides exercises for many of the clairs, and may present as a tool towards that end.

As examples are a testament to the "proof is in the pudding" philosophy, here is an example of the utilization of both pendulum, meditation and Claircognizance.

Ex. 9.1

A beautiful kitten named Geo, who is also on the feral side, was ill. While attempting to take her to the veterinarian over the course of two weeks, which was extremely difficult because she was to spry to catch, meditation and the pendulum were consulted over the same time frame.

Initially, it took a little under two days to notice she was actually not herself. By day three a friend, pet-store owner and former vet-tech was consulted. Antibiotics were recommended and a visit to the veterinarian. As this particular feline companion is considered to be the most precious of all time, the pendulum was consulted to help ease the mind. The result, she needed to go to the vet for an examination and tests.

On day three, she began antibiotic treatment, which proved to be extremely difficult to administer. It caused a disconnect in the human to feline relationship. Meditation to calm the mind and help with the feline stress was integrated. Meditation and medication had excellent results. She began to feel better and an appointment was made with the vet for Geo to be seen after antibiotic treatment was completed. This would help to verify if she had fully recovered or if there was something more serious that needed a different type of medication.

On day seven, an attempt was made to take Geo to the vet. Due to a mistrust that developed during antibiotic treatment, she wouldn't allow herself to be captured. After feeling better for a few days, her illness continued to the point where she stopped being her loving and playful self along with loss of appetite. Meditation continued and another consult with the pendulum occurred. The questions were: **1.** Is Geo still ill?; **2.** If "Yes," will she not recover without treatment? The results were both in the affirmative. During deep breathing exercises and meditation, intuition clicked in. It was an overwhelming feeling that, if Geo didn't see a veterinarian, she wouldn't survive. The pendulum results indicated that the local mobile vet would be easier than attempting a capture. She was telephoned and expected to visit by day twelve.

Mediation continued, with healing exercises incorporated. Geo's health continued to decline. On day twelve, the mobile vet arrived on time but Geo would not come out from under the bed. An hour passed and the mobile vet stated that she would need to reschedule. During the conversation, she advised that there was an emergency veterinary clinic about an hour away that would be more helpful and, if necessary, Geo could be sedated in order to run the necessary tests. During the next hour, calls were made to a friend, pet store proprietor and former vet-tech extraordinaire, in an attempt to figure a way to retrieve Geo. She was finally able to rescue Geo, allowing a trip to the vet clinic a little under an hour away. A thorough examination and tests were completed, leaving the answers to Geo's ailments with the necessary steps to be taken in order for a full recovery.

The true point of the story is to understand that *everyone* can have access and answers to *any* given situation but they must follow their intuition. The pendulum is a great regulation tool, as is meditation, both assist with quieting the mind, therefore, the soul. If the indication that the mobile vet was not the next course of action, the information regarding the emergency veterinary clinic would never have come to light. That small piece of the puzzle was an essential requirement for complete resolution. It is about trusting the process of the information that is being brought forth. Some would say "having faith." It also helps to have others with which one can rely.

CHAPTER 10

AKASHIC RECORDS

Akasha is a Sanskrit word, meaning *"primary substance,"* which is taken from the Introduction to *The Aquarian Gospel of Jesus the Christ* by Levi H. Dowling (1908). This *primary substance* "...is the first stage of the crystallization of spirit," for which all things are shaped. Being of such an "exquisite fineness" and "so sensitive to the slightest vibrations," the Universe registers this energy with "...an indelible impression" that continues beyond space and time. It is liken to the concept of registering one's decisions every second of every minute of every day. According to Theosophy, and its connection to the spiritual movement known as Anthroposophy, *Akasha* is also referred to as "aether," "sky," or "atmosphere," believed to be a comprehensive collection of "...universal events, thoughts, words, emotions, and intent ever to have occurred in the past, present, or future in terms of all entities and life forms, not just humans."[37] All knowledge is stored within the ethereal realm of the Akashic Records. Eastern thought, through the eyes of 15th Century Swiss philosopher Paracelsus, refers to "A'kasa" as an invisible and intangible living primordial spiritual substance "...corresponding to the conception of some form of cosmic ether pervading [within] the solar system" (Hartmann, p. 17). In layman's terms, the Akashic Records are the *cosmic database* that contain *all* insight, knowledge and wisdom relating to the universe. Perhaps, even beyond. If one were to use their imagination, the Akashic Records would appear as a vast library, the size of which exceeds the magnitude of several planets within the Milky Way galaxy. Additionally, these records are open to *anyone* who is pure of heart. That is the key to learning how to access past, present and future

---

[37] See Ervin László works concerning his theory of quantum consciousness.

personal information, as well as that of friends, family and other cosmic beings. Many psychics can, and often do, literally *stream* data from this particular origin while conducting their particular brand of readings.

Some authorities claim these records are located on the Astral Plane, or Fourth Dimensional plane of time and space. Others, however, believe said records exist at the Eighth Dimensional plane of existence with the Twelfth Dimensional plane being the highest before reconnecting with Source.[38] Several experts in the field have their own take. Author Linda Howe, in her famous book, *How to Read the Akashic Records, Accessing the Archive of the Soul and Its Journey*, states "Akashic wisdom comes from outside of, or beyond, the self" (p. 59). She believes access is allowed for *all* who seek divine knowledge and understanding of the universe. This incredibly vast level of information relates to "...a perspective that spans the universe and covers every lifetime that [*every*] soul has ever lived" (p. 59). Well-renowned "ET Contactee, Ascension Coach & Galactic Historian" Debbie Solaris on the other hand states, "[t]he Akashic Records are an energetic library of information that contains the collective consciousness of all souls throughout time and space. They are a source of divine knowledge and understanding that can be accessed by anyone who is willing to open their heart and mind to the wisdom of the universe. The purpose of the Akashic Records is to provide guidance and insight into our lives, our relationships, and our spiritual journey" (Galactic Akashic Records Course; Week 1 – "What is the purpose of the Akashic Records?"). Solaris adds that, in order for one to gain access into this boundless library of knowledge, "you must first create a sacred space...by lighting a candle, burning incense, or playing calming music." Meditation, prayer and the implementation of sound via chanting or use of singing bowls, or simply sitting still, are all excellent ways to tap into this "Book of Life." The other notable reference utilized, and for which there are many sacred text references, Biblical and otherwise. Lastly, Akashic Records Instructor Maria Elena Mexia[39] explains her view of the "Akasha" as being an "...all-pervasive, all-encompassing existence," that creates every visible and invisible form, as well as everything that

---

[38] The Milky Way galaxy is only a part of this particular Universe's existence, wherein the highest dimensional realm in this galaxy concludes at the 13th dimension where Source resides. Other Universes have different levels of dimensional existence.
[39] Excerpt taken from online Akashic Records course, Level 1 Manual.

falls under our senses. Really, "[i]t is the omnipresent spiritual force that permeates the universe. The Akasha is a plane of unlimited existence of knowledge in which all universal memories are imbued and stored" (Mexia[39]).

There are differences of opinion regarding "who" is actually in charge of such an important realm. Linda Howe bases her particular observations upon a more Christ consciousness viewpoint. She refers to those who manage the Akashic Records as the "Lords of the Records." A phrase that indicates one who studies and believes, wholeheartedly, in the ideology of Christianity. Howe states, with utter precision, that the Lords of the Records are Light Beings of unity consciousness who "...are responsible for maintaining the integrity and incorruptibility of the Akashic Records" (p. 42). She also discusses the concept of the Higher Self and Spirit Guides which tend to present themselves in the form of "Masters, Teachers and Love Ones." Said Guides, Howe believes, communicate with the Lords of the Records to provide accurate intel. Although it may appear difficult to comprehend, the use of symbols, numbers (numerology), archetypes and dreams represent the types of communication to be expected by one's Spirit Guides. Communication from one's Guides is person specific. In other words, they speak one's true language by providing information that is "personal" to that individual.

During Season 1, Episode 1, of Matias de Stephano's phenomenal series *Initiation*, he defines the Akashic Records as "...a compendium of all events, thoughts, words, emotions and intent that have occurred in the past, present and future." Debbie Solaris' deep dive revealed to her that the Arcturians[40], an extraterrestrial race of enlightened and highly evolved ET's from the Boötes Constellation, are in charge of their maintenance and for granting access. Arcturians operate under unity consciousness, not individuality per se. While Solaris initially utilizes the same terminology (i.e., "the Lords of the Records") in her teachings, she elaborates further, drawing upon her own personal experience and knowledge. Other Galactic Akashic Records Readers and spiritual teachers believe that beings from

---

[40] The Arcturians are an alien species that currently reside on the planet "Arcturus" in the Boötes, or the Herdsman constellation. This group of "alien" beings are highly evolved, advanced 12th Dimensional beings that present in crystalline form when visible to the fortunate here on Earth.

Antares are the primary guardians. In some circles, Archangel Metatron has also been claimed as a guardian. Regardless of the question of *who,* consensus from all remains clear: The beings in charge are of the Light. The ultimate goal for learning to access the Akashic Records is to provide a deep insight into the authenticity of self and one's inherent intuitive or psychic aptitude, as well as opening the mind with pure clarity into one's past, present and future.

Another well known author, Dolores Cannon, has her own special story to add to the intrigue. She began her career as a hypnotherapist for the purpose of helping those suffering from childhood trauma find coping mechanisms and techniques designed for release. While under hypnosis, Cannon discovered that one of her patient's was not speaking of her present-day life but began speaking as if she was on Earth but during a different era. To verify this revelation, she began asking questions. She discovered that her client's references were no longer associated with the 20th Century. This breakthrough began her own personal research into past life regression sessions with other willing participants. Eventually, she gathered enough evidence that she could no longer deny the truth. Something, beyond present day Earth based knowledge, was happening. Over the course of several years her research lead to the discovery of the Akashic Records, which she believed could be accessed by every person through their own personal connection with their Higher Self, and was deeply embedded in the subconscious[41] mind. In 1968, Cannon and her husband Johnny discovered that not just one past life presented but several. In order to share her findings with others, she created the Quantum Healing Hypnosis Technique foundation that is still active today, ten years after her death. During her later years of hypnosis therapy and study, the introduction to Inter Planetary Beings ("IP's" or "IPB's) came to the forefront, promoting a new set of books for which Cannon is also famous.

While it is said that anyone can access the Akashic Records, it is easier if one builds a foundation before attempting access. This begins with taking a specific set of steps. The first step is to *know thyself,* which

---

[41] The subconscious mind has been referred to by other spiritual teachers as The OverSoul, Christ Consciousness, Higher Consciousness, the Universal Mind and Oneness with Source.

takes a certain amount of maturity. This may entail going beyond the social mores that have been taught since early childhood. It does not, however, infer that one should disregard all of what has been taught on a cultural and societal basis. It simply means that one must be discerning. Discernment refers to one's ability to be able to perceive, recognize and apprehend knowledge through observation or via their intellect. In other words, the development of good judgment must be present. The second step requires one to begin connecting with their Higher Self – the part of you that exists within your subconscious while also being awake. Author, Elizabeth Clare Prophet likens the Higher Self to being at one with all creation and having a deep connection to a spiritual sun (Source), for which we are all connected. Your true essence is "...concentrated light, energy and consciousness, bursting with potential" (p. 7). The disconnection that developed over many millennia created a shadow between oneself and Source. For some souls, the veil is thin, allowing remembrance through each lifetime to be a simple task. Through the etheric fields of consciousness, the Higher Self can see the world from a completely different perspective, opening up the mind, and therefore consciousness, to what is truly life changing. For others, the veil can be so thick that remembering one's Higher Self seems nearly impossible. Those experiencing more darkness than light have fallen deeper into the sleep state "...forgetting [his/her/their] origins and [his/her/their] potential to create as God creates" (p. 9). The Higher Self must be activated. Step three requires letting go of preconceived notions of reality. While one's soul chooses to reside on Earth, or the Third Dimensional plane, it is limited to what goes beyond matter. All that is "seen" continues throughout time and space, which is considered Fourth Dimensional existence. These dimensions are inextricably linked and can not exist independently of one another. It is likened to the phrase "Stepping outside the box." Be open to the infinite. Step four requires the centering of one's energetic body or field, which continues outward approximately seven feet in all directions from the physical body. (See Chapter 1, *Chakras*.) Advanced souls who are connected to their Authentic Self, the "real" self without ego, can extend their auric field exponentially, sending their energy field outward, ten fold over the standard seven. This is possible because the Records work

113

in tandem with vibration and energetic frequencies. One must be truly open to all that remains unknown or appears impossible.

Accessing the Akashic Records is a purposeful endeavor. It helps one gain an understanding of their multidimensional self; the self that has gained an understanding of their purpose. It acts as a guide to help one reach their greatest potential and open the doors to possibilities beyond belief, which is a truly a remarkable gift.

CHAPTER 11

REINCARNATION

Pursuant to the discussion regarding the topic of "energy" in Chapter 1, the human body is basically derived of energy that encases consciousness (a/k/a, the soul or essence). Chapter 10 discusses that energy is considered a *primary substance*, which "...is the first stage of the crystallization of spirit," for which all things are shaped. While life and death are the polarity of what appears to be our finite existence, in truth, we are infinite fragments of the same Source. "There is an invisible universe within the visible one, a world of causes within the world of effects," for which "...the world of the soul and the realms of the spirit can only be known" to one "...whose inner senses are awakened to life" (Hartmann, p. vii). Consciousness begins in the mind; the "I AM" principle. Consciousness is an awareness and spiritual perception of the soul, which brings us to the subject of Reincarnation.

More religions extant on Earth today, many inherently and without question, believe in the concept of reincarnation than do not. From the perennial philosophers perspective, specifically 15th Century BCE, philosophy and spirituality viewed religious traditions as a sharing of a single, metaphysical truth or origin from which all esoteric knowledge and doctrine was derived.[42] Madame Helena Blavatsky, a 19th Century occultist[43], as paraphrased by Elizabeth Kim, believed that, "[a]t its core

---

[42] Reference derived from *The Perennial Philosophy* by Aldous Huxley, published in 1945.

[43] An "Occultist" is not a member of a "Cult!" The meaning of the word *Occultist*, as defined by Dictionary.com, is "...a person who believes in or practices occult arts, such as magic, astrology, alchemy, seances, or other activity claiming the use of secret knowledge or supernatural powers or agencies."

[the underlying] belief in a truth underlying all religions…" is "a sense of union…" with Source. She adds that "…true knowledge does not come to a person via the senses, or through reason, but through direct contact with the divine" (p. 64). Cultures in South America and Africa have always incorporated the idea that "God" (a/k/a, "The All," "All That Is," "Creator," "Everything That Is," "Source," "Tao," "Yahweh," "Great Spirit," etc.) is the *Creator* of all that exists. This is the *one* common cultural thread amongst all humans beings. Reincarnation is also a factor of *The Kybalion*, an ancient Egyptian text wherein the Seven Principles of the Universe are explained. Whether or not one believes in reincarnation does not preclude its certainty. "A leaf does not have to believe in photosynthesis to turn green" (Yarboro, p. 27).

One of the most important facets of transformation is that there is no correct or incorrect way to evolve, "for that would mean there was an eternal 'authority' whose choice superseded your own" (Michael, New Final Comments, Yarboro, July 2004). Additionally, how unjust would the world be if only one lifetime were allowed? "What good would it do us to work, suffer, and strive to perfect the beautiful things…if we were not permitted to return to enjoy the fruits of our efforts?" (Ward, pg. 71) Better yet, what recourse would there be for those who have caused harm to others by taking away one's *free will* to choose their own path? Evolution is a personal path for every soul, which is the accumulation of many lifetimes on Earth, elsewhere in the Universe, even beyond. One's journey is just that, a personal path back to Source with its own twists and turns through the myriad of possibilities and intentions. All such "choices" embody *free will*, which ultimately refers to the principle of cause and effect. According to Matias de Staphano, "[y]ou are the cause of everything that effects you in your life" (de Stephano, 2019) [S1; Ep7]. This statement is also a reflection of the Seven Principles of the Universe.

As stated long ago in the Bhagavad-Gita, which is often referred to as "The Song of God" or "Song of the Lord," "[a]s a man, casting off warn-out garments…taketh new ones, so the dweller of the body, casting off worn-out bodies, entereth into others that are new. For sure is the death of him that is born, and sure the birth of him that is dead; therefore over the inevitable thou shoudst not grieve." Gautama Buddha, the Avatar[44] born several centuries before the birth of Christ, taught there was no escaping one's actions. For every *cause*, there is an equal and opposite *effect*. As a result of the polarity of our existence, actions must always have consequences, whether one believes their actions have consequences is of no concern to the Universe. All intentions, whether positive or negative, create one's circumstances. And "...without the cycle of rebirth life is meaningless and without purpose" (Montgomery, p. 10). Several centuries before the true indoctrination of Catholicism, the first organized Christian religion, Saint Augustine in 1:6 states: "Did I not live in another body, or somewhere else, before entering my mother's womb?" There are other Saints who came to the same conclusion. The ultimate goal for those of the Hindu faith is to reach *perfection*, which will lead them to Nirvana; oneness with the Creator. For Christians, it is to reach the Kingdom of Heaven, also the place of *perfection* wherein God resides. Are these beliefs so vastly different? The end goal is the same, to reach *perfection* before returning to the heart of Source, or becoming one with God.

There are also many highly intelligent famous people who endorse reincarnation over the "only one life to live" philosophy. Louisa May Alcott, Edgar Cayce, Thomas Edison, Ralph Waldo Emerson, Henry Ford, Benjamin Franklin, Carl Jung, Nikola Tesla and François Marie Voltaire to name a few. This brings us back to the questions asked by Ruth Montgomery in her book "Here and Hereafter," wherein upon opening the first page of her delightful book she asks: "Who has not experienced the eerie feeling, on glimpsing a village street or foreign seaport, that he has been there before?" Even better still: "Who has not met a stranger with whom he felt instant rapport, as if he had always known him, or taken a violent dislike for another before the introductions were even completed?" There are hundreds of thousands of accounts of past life recall, many of which were discovered under hypnosis. This was astonishing to both the therapist and the patient. One favorite explanation, again by Montgomery,

---

[44] In Hinduism, an "Avatar" is referred to a deity that descends onto earth form as the human form of Source. In Catholicism, the reference to "The Holy Trinity," and utilizing the sign of the cross "In the name of the Father, the Son and the Holy Ghost" makes the same reference for "God" appeared in human form as an Avatar to help guide humanity towards love and light.

states "[i]s God so whimsical and unloving that He plays favorites with His children, granting radiant health to one and misery to another..." (p. 12). Additionally, when one taps into their own Akashic Records, or has assistance through a credible Reader, they are able to see the past, present and, often times, even a glimpse of a potential future. Stories have been told about young children speaking foreign languages that are unknown to their parents, even grandparents. Another story reported by a young mother discusses how her four year old son would continually speak, and even draw pictures, of a specific mechanical device connected to a large ship (The Titanic!) that was created nearly 100 years before his birth. Many people report having dreams of being in foreign countries, wherein they were able to both speak and understand the native tongue of origin without any past history of the country. Many with incredibly intricate details of the buildings, clothing and scenery. The explanation – they were (re) experiencing a past life. In some instances, these stories can even be verified.

Of course, there is always the usual questions: "Why can't I remember?" and "What would be the significance of remembering something that happened ages ago?" The existence and evolution of humans has been occurring for millions, even billions of years, and at a rather slow pace. According to historians, the earth is approximately 4.5 billion years old. It has been estimated that Homo sapiens have been on earth for 300,000+ years. That is a whole lot of lifetimes to live! Let's ponder some explanations directly related to the "why" one can't remember.

The premise: If one has lived several past lives on earth, perhaps even lives on other planets within our galaxy, why are we unable to remember? First and foremost, not every life lived has a chain reaction to the current one. The entire purpose for the creation of Earth, including all its inhabitants, is based upon these simple principle; to experience polarity and explore the immensity of creativity through *free will*. Each century, or decade for that matter, offers evolution and expansion. Hopefully, with the end result having each person grow closer towards perfection. That is, the perfection of one's Authentic Self. This begs the question: How does one actually intentionally remember prior lives?

There are several techniques one can utilize to reach the answers to the above question. The first response is a familiar one: Meditation. As postulated in Chapter 9, this is also the key to opening one's intuition and/or psychic abilities. Once one has gleaned their essence (a/k/a, sub-or super-consciousness) and becomes aware of both their Higher Self and Guides for assistance, checking in to verify past lives becomes easier. Many may need validation; however, practice creates intention and allows information to become more clear. Be open to the information that flows and how it resonates with your soul. Past life recall can present within the dream state, or actually become apparent during travel to a specific locale. Perhaps, even through a feeling, or an inclination, after hearing about a far off place through a friend, family member, even the media. That specific geographical location suddenly becomes familiar, and is usually accompanied by a detailed description of the surrounding landscape.

Ward describes reincarnation as the process of being "...given a new body, new environment, new family connections and a different life influence..." during each incarnation (p. 71). This gives a new meaning to "family ties." It presents a conundrum, for *all* your past actions during any lifetime, again, have consequences; cause and effect. One just can't escape it. Ward also claims that "...no personality is completely reborn" (p. 17). There are always remnants of one's essence that continues from lifetime to lifetime. The journey toward the understanding of *All That Is* can also be expedited when one participates within the realm of "Service to Others." In turn, this also promotes less drama, therefore, less trauma. Yes, many life lessons are difficult, usually due to one's ego; however, if one approaches the world through a Service to Others lens, rather than a "Service to Self," they will be pleasantly surprised at how quickly their life becomes easier, less stressful, less daunting and fearful.

Another technique was provided to Ruth Montgomery through her own Guides. This requires a trip down memory lane. Through automatic writing, her Guides offered the following insight: "When you think back to certain aspects of your childhood which stand out as unique, see if you will remember something else that seemed to have promulgated that situation for which there seemed no explanation" (pp. 20-21). By recalling these oddities, through sight, sound and emotions, the understanding of childhood events become clearer, thus helping with the recollection of early days before one became immersed in their current lifetime. "As a starter, one could simply recall a past experience which made an unusual impact, such as doorway that seemed familiar, the tantalizing aroma of a flower not previously encountered, or the yearning for a particular fragrance or taste" (Montgomery. p. 21). Journaling is also a great way to recapture experiences without over analyzing. Write it down as it presents, analyze it later. Look for patterns as well. Through analysis of the information received one can begin to understand "...what has influenced our present course of action, what errors of commission or omission we are here to rectify and what good we accomplished from which we are now reaping benefit" (Montgomery, p. 22). Under Hermetic Teachings, reincarnation occurs within all the worlds contained throughout the Universes. Worlds, along with all living things, "...are born, grow and die; only to be reborn" (*The* Kybalion, Three Initiates, Centenary Edition, p. 102). This is akin to the seasons of winter, spring, summer and fall.

What would be the significance of having past life recall knowledge? There are several. In this vast journey of existence through polarity, duality, exploration and expansion, remembering comes in handy when faced with challenging situations. One could even say a bit of wisdom comes through, allowing for a view of the whole picture, not just facets. This is also a theme of *this* life's primary existence. We are born and continually learn from infancy. As we age, one can only hope that wisdom will follow. If one cares to *really* look at their progression, patterns become apparent. Repetitive forms of behavior that anchor themselves on the negative polarity are an indication that growth in the opposite direction is essential. Where one has walked before creates a better perspective of current action. The underlying requirement for evolution *is* remembrance. It leads the student into the light of knowledge, compassion and understanding, thereby ending the cyclical nature of repeating the same, unwanted behavior.

This chapter cannot end without a final Biblical reference. One would be hard pressed in today's society to find someone who has not heard the Old Testament pronouncement, "An eye for an eye; a tooth for a tooth," along with the unmistakable statement in Revelations, "He that leadeth into captivity shall go into captivity; he that killeth with the sword must be killed by the sword." During the time frame in which these specific words were written, leads one to take into account the actual words chosen. They are not "literal" in the sense that, if some kills someone with a sword, they must receive the same type of death. It is the principle of the matter, referencing the laws of cause and effect. It would be impossible for every misdeed, or beautiful gesture of kindness, to be repaid in one lifetime. It simply is not humanly possible.

CONCLUSION

Providing the foregoing insights into these Metaphysical topics has been a pleasure. The importance of each topic is to engage the public in forward thinking. To take a deep dive into philosophical and spiritual domains. The consciousness of Earth, as well as all its inhabitants, is embarking on an increased change in awareness. One that purports, even propels, one toward a more spiritual understanding of human existence. The pivotal moment started when the Age of Aquarius – expansion, replaced the Age of Pisces – victimization. In astrological terms, a "new age" is a shift in consciousness that deeply affects humanity. General analyses and consensus is that each new time period brings about the rise and fall of civilizations and/or cultural tendencies. Unity consciousness, wherein humans work together as a species, is the wave of the future. Taking the current mindset into a higher dimensional understanding is also on the docket.

It is easy to fall into the trap of "doom and gloom," especially in light of recent events throughout the world in which we live. Many cultures, through governmental regime, promote and incorporate a fear based existence. This is a form of control that has been the mainstay of society for far too long. Humans are smarter than this. It is time to awaken.

REFERENCES & ADDITIONAL SOURCES

BOOK REFERENCES

Brown, A. and Brown, N. *Fairy Wisdom Oracle Deck & Book Set.* U. S. Games Systems, Inc., 2020.

Dispenza, Joe. *Supernatural Humans: How Common People Are Doing the Uncommon.* Hay House, Inc., Carlsbad, CA, 2017.

Dowling, Levi H. *The Aquarian Gospel of Jesus the Christ.* Publisher, 1908.

Eason, Cassandra. *A Little Bit of Palmistry.* Sterling Ethos, New York *USA,* 2018.

Hartmann, Franz. *The Life and Doctrines of Paracelsus.* Kshetra Books, USA, 2016. Original Publication by Franz Hartmann, M. D. in 1891.

Howe, Linda. *How to Read the Akashic Records, Accessing the Archive of the Soul and Its Journey.* Sounds True, Inc., Boulder, CO, 2009.

Huxley, Aldous. *The Perennial Philosophy: An Interpretation of the Great Mystics, East and West.* Harper & Brothers, USA, 1945.

Kim, Elizabeth. *Spiritus Mundi.* Liminal 11, 2022.

Lau, Theodora. *Chinese Horoscopes Guide to Relationship.* Doubleday, 1995.

Montgomery, Ruth. *Here and Hereafter.* Fawcett Publications, Inc., 1968.

Parkyn, Chetan. *Human Design: Discover the Person You Were Born to Be.* *Harper Collins UK,* 2010.

Prophet, Elizabeth Clare. *Access The Power Of Your Higher Self.* Summer Publications, Inc., 1997.

Riso, Don Richard & Hudson, Russ. *The Wisdom of the Enneagram: The Complete Guide to Psychological and Spiritual Growth for the Nine Personality Types.* Random House Publishing Group, 1999.

Robbins, Heather Roan. *Starcodes Astro Oracle.* Hay House, Inc., 2021.

Royal-Holt, Lyssa. *Galactic Heritage Cards.* Light Technology Publishing, LLC, Flagstaff, AZ, 2013.

Royal-Holt, Lyssa. *The Prism of Lyra.* Light Technology Publishing, 1989.

Rudd, Richard. *The Gene Keys: Embracing Your Higher Purpose.* Watkins Publishing, 2013.

Segal, Inna. *Mystical Healing Reading Cards.* Rockpool Publishing, 2020.

Smoley, Richard. *The Kybalion, Hermetic Philosophy.* A TarcherPerigee Book. An Imprint of Penguin Random LLC, 2018.

Star, Dean. *The Astrocartography Handbook. The Beginner's Guide to Astrocartography.* Self-Published 2024.

Touchkoff, Svetlana Alexandrovna. *Russian Gypsy Fortune Telling Cards.* HarperOne, 1991.

Ward, Margarete. *Gong Hee Fot Choy.* Celestial Arts, 2009.

Yarboro, Chelsea Quinn. *Messages from Michael.* Playboy Press, 1979.

WEBSITE REFERENCES

Solaris, Debbie. 2024. Eight Week Class on *Galactic Akashic Records*. Accessed 1 April 2024 through 31 May 2024. All reference to Ms. Solaris are derived from this extensive course and her website: DebbieSolaris.com.

Silverberg, L. M. & Eischen, J. 2020. *The Conversation* website. Accessed 3, Feb. 2024. (Specifically, "https://*www.fragments-of-energy-not-waves-or-particles-may-be-the-fundamental-building-blocks-of-the-universe*-150730.")

Stelter, Gretchen. 2016. *The Beginner's Guide to the 7 Chakras and Their Meanings*. Healthline.com. Accessed 20 March 2020.

"Deluxe Numerology Report ~ Kimberly James." Numerology.com. Accessed 10 April 2024.

"Einstein's Big Idea." 2005. pbs.org/. Accessed 21 Feb. 2024.

"History of Energy." 2022. en.wikipedia.org/. Accessed 7 Jan. 2024.

"Tarot and Oracle Cards: What's The Difference?" 2019. Modified 2020. www.thegoddesselite.com. Accessed 7 April 2024.

"The Aura – Your Energy Counterpart." 2011. www.aetherius.org. Accessed 19 Feb. 2024.

"The Pendulum." 2024. www.britannica.com/technology/pendulum. Accessed 23 Feb. 2024.

"Who invented playing cards and what is the origin of 'Hearts', 'Diamonds', 'Clubs' and 'Spades'?" 2011. guardian.co.uk. Accessed 10 April 2024.

Printed in the United States
by Baker & Taylor Publisher Services